AEROSPACE AGENCIES AND ORGANIZATIONS

AEROSPACE AGENCIES AND ORGANIZATIONS

A GUIDE FOR BUSINESS AND GOVERNMENT

George V. d'Angelo

QUORUM BOOKS
Westport, Connecticut • London

Library of Congress Cataloging-in-Publication Data

d'Angelo, George V.
    Aerospace agencies and organizations : a guide for business and
government / George V. d'Angelo.
       p. cm.
    Includes index.
    ISBN 0–89930–842–2 (alk. paper)
    1. Aerospace industries. I. Title.
HD9711.5.D36 1993
338.7′6291′025—dc20   93–293

British Library Cataloguing in Publication Data is available.

Library of Congress Catalog Card Number: 93–293
ISBN: 0–89930–842–2

First published in 1993

Quorum Books, 88 Post Road West, Westport, CT 06881
An imprint of Greenwood Publishing Group, Inc.

Printed in the United States of America

The paper used in this book complies with the
Permanent Paper Standard issued by the National
Information Standards Organization (Z39.48–1984).

10 9 8 7 6 5 4 3 2 1

For I dipped into the future, far as human eye could see, saw the vision of the world, and all the wonder it would be.

Alfred, Lord Tennyson, 1842

Contents

Abbreviations

ACC	Advisory Committee on Co-ordination
ACRES	Australian Center for Remote Sensing
ACSTD	Advisory Committee for Science and Technology for Development
AIAA	American Institute of Aeronautics and Astronautics
AIST	Agency of Industrial Science and Technology (Japan)
ALCORSS	Australian Liaison Committee on Remote Sensing by Satellite
ANSTP	Austrian National Space Technology Program
ARABSAT	Arab Satellite Communication Organization
ARSP	African Regional Remote Sensing Program
ASA	Austrian Space Agency
ASC	American Space Council
ASI	Agenzia Spaziale Italiana
ASR	Romanian Space Agency
ASTRA	Application of Space Techniques Relating to Aviation
AUSLIG	Australian Surveying and Land Information Group
AVA	Aerodynamische Veruchsanstalt
BCRS	Netherlands Remote Sensing Board
BDT	Telecommunications Development Bureau
BIMDA	Bioserve ITA Materials Apparatus

BMFT	Federal Ministry for Research and Technology
BWYIC	Beijing Wang Yuan Industry Corporation
CAeM	WMO Commission for Aeronautical Meteorology
CAgM	WMO Commission for Agricultural Meteorology
CASP	Center for Advanced Space Propulsion
CAST	Chinese Academy of Space Technology
CCDS	Centers for the Commercial Development of Space
CCIR	International Radio Consultative Committee
CCITT	International Telegraph and Telephone Consultative Committee
CDAS	Command and Data Acquisition Station (Japan)
CDSCC	Canberra Deep Space Communication Complex
CES	Coast Earth Station
CGWIC	China Great Wall Industry Corporation
CIS	Commonwealth of Independent States
CLS	Collecte et Localisation par Satellite
CLTC	China Satellite Launch and TT&C General
CNES	Centre National d'Études Spatiales
CNR	Centro Nazionale per la Ricerca
CNRS	Centre National de la Recherche Scientifique
COMSAT	Communication Satellite Corporation
COPUOS	Committee on the Peaceful Uses of Outer Space
COSMIC	Computer Software Management and Information Center
COSPAR	Committee on Space Research of ICSU
COSTED	Committee on Science and Technology in Developing Countries
CRAS	Romanian Commission for Space Activities
CRL	Communications Research Laboratory (Japan)
CRRES	Combined Release and Radiation Effects Satellite
CSA	Computer Sciences of Australia
CSDB	Central Specialized Design Bureau (Russia)
CSG	Guaiana Space Center
CSIRO	Commonwealth Scientific and Industrial Research Organization (Australia)
CST	Toulouse Space Center
DALI	Device to Access and Look at Spot Imagery
DARA	German Space Agency

DARPA	Defense Advanced Research Projects Agency
DESD	Department for Economic and Social Development
DFD	German Remote Sensing Data Center
DFVLR	German Aerospace Research Establishment
DGA	Délégation Générale pour l'Armement
DISA	Defense Information Systems Agency
DLR	German Aerospace Research Establishment
DMA	Defense Mapping Agency
DPC	Data Processing Center (Japan)
DRA	Defence Research Agency (United Kingdom)
DTI	Department of Trade and Industry (United Kingdom)
DTM	National Digital Terrain Model (China)
DoD	Department of Defense
DoE	Department of the Environment (United Kingdom)
EARSeL	European Association of Remote Sensing Laboratories
ECA	Economic Commission for Africa
ECOSOC	Economic and Social Council
ECSL	European Center of Space Law
ECU	European Currency Unit
ELDO	European Organization for the Development and Construction of Space Vehicle Launchers
ENRI	Electronic Navigation Research Institute (Japan)
EODC	Earth Observation Data Centre (United Kingdom)
EPO	Earthnet Program Office
EPTA	United Nations Expanded Program for Technical Assistance
ESA	European Space Agency
ESCAP	Economic and Social Commission for Asia and the Pacific
ESCO	European Satellite Consulting Organization
ESOC	European Space Operations Center
ESRIN	European Space Research Institute
ESRO	European Space Research Organization
ESTEC	European Space Research and Technology Center
ETL	Electrotechnical Laboratory (Japan)
EUMETSAT	European Meteorological Satellite Organization

EUTELSAT	European Telecommunications Satellite Organization
FAO	Food and Agriculture Organization of the United Nations
FCC	Federal Communications Commission
FCR	France Cables and Radio
FLTSATCOM	Fleet Satellite Communications
FORIS	Forest Resource Data Base
GARP	Global Atmosphere Research Program
GAS	Get Away Specials
GDTA	Groupement pour le Développement de la Télédetection Aérospatiale
GEMS	Global Environmental Monitoring System
GIS	Geographic Information Systems
GMS	Geostationary Meteorological Satellite
GPALS	Global Protection Against Limited Strikes
GSOC	German Space Operations Centre
GWE	Global Weather Experiment
HARV	High Alpha Research Vehicle
HIDEC	Highly Integrated Digital Electronic Control
HSR	High-Speed Research
IAA	International Academy of Astronautics
IACG	Inter-Agency Consultative Group for Space Science
IAEA	International Atomic Energy Agency
IAF	International Astronautical Federation
IAG	International Association of Geodesy
IAGA	International Association of Geomagnetism and Aeronomy
IAHS	International Association of Hydrological Sciences
IAMAP	International Association of Meteorology and Atmosphere Physics
IASPO	International Association of Physical Sciences of the Oceans
IATA	International Air Transport Association
IAU	International Astronomical Union
IBRD	International Bank for Reconstruction and Development
ICAO	International Civil Aviation Organization

ICRP	International Commission on Radiological Protection
ICSU	International Council of Scientific Unions
ICSU	International Council of Space Unions
IFRB	International Frequency Registration Board
IFREMER	French Institute of Marine Research
IGCSTD	Intergovernmental Committee on Science and Technology for Development
IGN	Institut Géographique National
IGOSS	Integrated Global Ocean Services System
ILO	International Labour Organization
IMO	International Maritime Organization
INMARSAT	International Maritime Satellite Organization
INTELSAT	International Telecommunications Satellite Organization
INTERSPUTNIK	International Organization of Space Communications
INMARSAT	International Maritime Satellite Organization
IRF	Swedish Institute of Space Physics
IRS	Information Retrieval Center
ISAS	Institute of Space and Astronautical Science (Japan)
ISCS	Interdisciplinary Scientific Commissions (COSPAR)
ISRO	Indian Space Research Organization
ISU	International Space University Organization
ITA	Instrumentation Technology Associates
ITC	International Institute for Aerospace Surveys and Earth Sciences
ITU	International Telecommunication Union
IUGG	International Union of Geodesy and Geophysics
JMA	Japan Meteorological Agency
KDD	Kokusai Denshin Denwa
KLM	Royal Dutch Airlines
KNMI	Royal Netherlands Meteorological Institute
KSC	Kagoshima Space Center
MAP	Middle Atmosphere Program
MDA	Materials Dispersion Apparatus
MEL	Mechanical Engineering Laboratory (Japan)

MILSTAR	Military Strategic and Tactical Relay System
MITI	Ministry of International Trade and Industry (Japan)
MOD	Ministry of Defence (United Kingdom)
MONSEE	Monitoring the Sun-Earth Environment
MOT	Ministry of Transport (Japan)
MPT	Ministry of Posts and Telecommunications
MRI	Meteorological Research Institute (Japan)
MRST	Ministry for the Coordination of Scientific and Technological Research (Italy)
MSA	Maritime Safety Agency (Japan)
MSC	Meteorological Satellite Center (Japan)
NAL	National Aerospace Laboratory (Japan)
NASA	National Aeronautics and Space Administration (United States)
NASC	National Aeronautics and Space Council (United Kingdom)
NASDA	National Space Development of Japan
NASP	National Aerospace Plane
NATO	North Atlantic Treaty Organization
NCAR	National Center for Atmospheric Research
NCS	Network Coordination Stations
NERC	Natural Environment Research Council (United Kingdom)
NHK	Japan Broadcasting Corporation
NICS	NATO Integrated Communication System
NIVR	Netherlands Agency for Aerospace Programs
NLR	National Aerospace Laboratory (The Netherlands)
NOAA	National Oceanic and Atmospheric Administration
NPS	Nuclear Power Source
NRO	National Reconnaissance Office
NRSC	National Remote Sensing Centre (China)
NSA	National Security Agency
NSF	National Science Foundation
NTA	Norwegian Telecommunications Administration
NTT	Nippon Telegraph and Telephone
NWO	Netherlands Organization for Scientific Research
OCC	Operations Control Center
OSC	Office of Space Commerce

OSC	Orbital Science Corporation
PIRC	Policy Implementation and Review Committee
PTT	Post Telephone and Telegraph
RAE	Royal Aerospace Establishment (United Kingdom)
RAL	Rutherford Appleton Laboratory
RRSP	Regional Remote Sensing Program
RSADU	Remote Sensing Applications Development Unit (United Kingdom)
RSRE	Royal Signals and Radar Establishment (United Kingdom)
SAC	Space Activities Commission (Japan)
SAMSO	Space and Missile Systems Organization
SCAR	Scientific Committee on Antarctic Research
SCC	Satellite Control Center
SCOPE	Scientific Committee on Problems of the Environment
SCOR	Scientific Committee on Oceanic Research
SCOSTEP	Scientific Committee on Solar-Terrestrial Physics
SDI	Strategic Defense Initiative
SDIO	Strategic Defense Initiative Organization
SERC	Science and Engineering Research Council (United Kingdom)
SES	Ship Earth Station
SFCG	Space Frequency Coordination Group
SFS	Space Frontier Society
SFU	Space Flyer Unit (Japan)
SHBOA	Shanghai Bureau of Astronautics
SIDCS	Space Industry Development Centers (Australia)
SINTEF	Foundation for Scientific and Industrial Research at the Norwegian Institute of Technology
SMA	Solar Maximum Analysis
SNSB	Swedish National Space Board
SPO	Science Policy Office
SPPS	Scientific Policy Planning Services
SRON	Space Research Organization of the Netherlands
SSC	Swedish Space Corporation
STA	Science and Technology Agency (Japan)

STEAR	Strategic Technologies in Automation and Robotics Program (Canada)
STOVL	Short Takeoff and Vertical Landing
TCD	Technical Cooperation for Development
TNO	Netherlands Organization for Applied Research
TSCJ	Telecommunications Satellite Corporation of Japan
TSS	Tromso Satellite Station
UAF	Upper Atmospheric Facilities
UN	United Nations
UNDP	United Nations Development Program
UNDRO	United Nations Disaster Relief Coordinator
UNEP	United Nations Environment Program
UNESCO	United Nations Educational, Scientific, and Cultural Organization
URSI	International Union of Radio Science
USAF	United States Air Force
WAFS	World Area Forecast System
WARC	World Administrative Radio Conference
WCAP	World Climate Applications Program
WCDP	World Climate Data Program
WCIP	World Climate Impacts Program
WCRP	World Climate Research Program
WDC	World Data Center
WGS	World Geodetic System
WHO	World Health Organization
WMO	World Meteorological Organization
WWF	World Wildlife Foundation
WWW	World Weather Watch Program

Introduction

"I believe that this nation should commit itself to achieving the goal, before this decade is over, of landing a man on the Moon and returning him safely to Earth." On May 25, 1961, President John F. Kennedy addressed these words of commitment to the U.S. Congress and the American people. When he spoke, the Soviet Union had already sent a man into orbit around the Earth, and the United States had launched a manned suborbital flight. The time seemed to have arrived for translating into reality an age-old dream of mankind—to have men leave their planetary cradle and stride on alien worlds.[1] At 9:32 A.M. eastern daylight time on July 16, 1969, the mission of Apollo 11 got under way. Approximately one million spectators in the Cape Kennedy, FL area and hundreds of millions of television viewers around the world watched the Saturn 5 rocket rise slowly from Launch Complex 39 with its manned Apollo payload.[2] On July 20, the Apollo 11 achieved the age-old dream. Two astronauts took the first steps on an alien world. Men had walked on the Moon.

The glamorous achievements of July 20, 1969, and all those that followed, did not happen by chance or overnight. They were the result of a long and complex technological evolution spurred by a variety of events and historical circumstances ranging from market forces to war.

Aerospace engineering may be said to have been born when the Wright brothers designed and built the first airplane in their bicycle shop in Dayton, OH, or when they flew it, on December 17, 1903. In the early years of development, aerospace engineering practices were largely borrowed from other fields. Civil engineering techniques were employed in analyzing airplane structures, and the first aircraft engines were designed with the assistance of automobile engineers. Aerodynamic design at this time was primarily empirical, although some liquid-flow concepts were obtained from marine sciences. Eventually, it was realized that effective aircraft engineering would require expanded knowledge of the basic technologies involved in flight. Thus aeronautical research groups were formed, such as the Aeromechanics Institute of Gottingen, Germany, in the early 1900s and the Advisory Committee for Aeronautics at the National Physics Laboratory in Great Britain in 1909.[3]

The word "aerospace" itself was originated by the U.S. Air Force when it began its initial research on flying vehicles that could operate in space as well as within the atmosphere. The term gained general usage in the early 1960s, concurrent with the development of a U.S. national space exploration program, when companies previously known for their work in aircraft felt the need to identify their capabilities in the rapidly expanding field of space technology.

The aerospace industry has gone through three major technical stages to evolve into its present size and scope: (1) the shift in construction materials in the 1930s, (2) the development of the gas turbine engine and the breakthrough to supersonic speeds in the late 1940s, and (3) the development of intercontinental ballistic missiles and the extension of its technology into space exploration in the late 1950s.

While some areas of aerospace research are adequately financed by private industry, other technologies, particularly those relating to space exploration, cannot be developed without substantial government funding and participation. Certain space activities will some day pay handsome dividends in terms of earth applications and benefits to mankind. Most private firms, however, cannot afford to invest huge amounts of money without a quantifiable return on their investment within a certain time frame. For that reason, every country active in the aerospace field benefits from government funding and direction, particularly where defense-related activities are involved.

In addition to the space agencies and related institutions at the national level, the United Nations and many Specialized Agencies, as well as other international organizations, have been involved in aerospace activities for decades. Those activities and the aerospace industry itself are regulated, coordinated, and stimulated by governments more than any other industry in the private sector. In order to analyze the aerospace industry and the related scientific and technological developments, it is therefore essential to understand the role played by all the public and quasi-public institutions involved.

This book is not concerned with the scientific and technical aspects of aerospace per se. It does not specifically deal with private sector research and development or manufacturing. All that is attempted here is a description of the international framework of public institutions that deal with aerospace activities and help make them possible.

Chapter One

The Space Powers

THE UNITED STATES

The National Space Council

On December 14, 1972, Gene Cernan left man's last footprint on the Moon. The Apollo program cost $100 billion in 1990 dollars and lasted eight years. During that time other, non-Apollo space efforts grew at unprecedented rates, the government hired the largest scientific force in history, and colleges and universities swelled with applicants and graduates in science and engineering. President Richard Nixon, however, decided against a follow-up exploration initiative to include a space station, a return to the Moon, or a manned journey to Mars. He started instead the space shuttle program as a "stepping stone" but made no commitments beyond that development. In 1984 President Ronald Reagan initiated the Space Station program as a means of "assuring for the United States preeminence in the utilization and exploration of space."

Early Congressional criticism of the Space Station focused on the lack of an overall plan and strategy. That criticism echoed a widely felt perception that a lack of long-term focus was a critical defect of the American space program.

The National Academy of Sciences wrote President-elect George Bush in December 1988 urging him to provide a long-term goal for space exploration: completion of Space Station Freedom before the end of the nineties, a return to the Moon to stay, and a human exploration of Mars. On April, 20 1989, by Executive Order No. 12675, President Bush established the National Space Council in order to coordinate U.S. space policies and strategies and to monitor their implementation. In signing the order, the president noted that space is of vital importance to the nation's future and to the quality of life on Earth, and he charged the council to keep America first in space.

The council is composed of the following members:

1. The vice president, who is chairman of the council;
2. The secretary of state;
3. The secretary of the treasury;
4. The secretary of defense;
5. The secretary of commerce;
6. The secretary of transportation;
7. The secretary of energy;
8. The director of the Office of Management and Budget;
9. The chief of staff to the president;
10. The assistant to the president for national security affairs;
11. The assistant to the president for science and technology;
12. The director of Central Intelligence; and
13. The administrator of the National Aeronautics and Space Administration.

From time to time, the chairman may also invite the chairman of the Joint Chiefs of Staff and the heads of other executive departments and agencies or senior officials to participate in the meetings of the council.

In addition to assisting the president on national space policy, the council also has the following functions:

- review United States government space policy, including long-range goals, and develop a strategy for national space activities;
- develop recommendations for the president on space policy and space-related issues;
- monitor and coordinate implementation of the objectives of the president's national space policy by executive departments and agencies; and
- foster close coordination, cooperation, and technology and information exchange among the civil, national security, and commercial space sectors, and facilitate resolution of differences concerning major space policy issues.

In accordance with the provisions of the Federal Advisory Committee Act, as amended (5 U.S.C. App. 2), the vice president establishes an advisory committee of private citizens to advise the vice president on the space policy of the United States (the "Board"). The vice president appoints the members of the board and designates a chairman. The executive secretary of the National Space Council serves as secretary to the board.

The executive secretary of the Council is appointed by the president. The council is also supported by a sub-cabinet-level interagency Policy Implementation and Review Committee (PIRC) composed of senior representatives of each member of the Space Council and chaired by the Space Council's executive secretary. Interagency working groups, chaired by Space Council staff, prepare policy studies, develop strategy alternatives, and provide advice and recommendations to the PIRC.

National Space Policy

According to an unclassified presidential document, dated November 2, 1989, the national space policy of the United States can be summarized as follows.

United States space activities are conducted by three separate and distinct sectors: two strongly interacting governmental sectors (civil and national security) and a separate, nongovernmental, commercial sector. Close coordination, cooperation, and information exchange should be maintained among these sectors to avoid unnecessary duplication and promote more efficient attainment of goals.

Goals and Principles. A fundamental objective guiding United States space activities is leadership. Leadership in an increasingly competitive international environment does not require United States preeminence in all areas and disciplines of space enterprise. It does, however, require preeminence in the key areas of space activity critical to achieving national security, scientific, technical, economic, and foreign policy goals.

The overall goals of U.S. space activities are: (1) to strengthen the security of the United States; (2) to obtain scientific, technological, and economic benefits for the general population and to improve the quality of life on Earth through space-related activities; (3) to encourage continuing United States private-sector investment in space-related activities; (4) to promote international cooperative activities, taking into account U.S. national security, foreign policy, scientific, and economic interests; (5) to cooperate with other nations in maintaining the freedom of space for all activities that enhance the security and welfare of mankind; and (6) as a long-range goal, to expand human presence and activity beyond Earth's orbit into the solar system.

Civil Space Policy. The United States civil space sector activities are to contribute significantly to enhancing the nation's science, technology, economy, pride, sense of well-being, and direction, as well as the United States' world prestige and leadership. Civil sector activities should comprise a balanced strategy of research, development, operations, and technology for science, exploration, and appropriate applications.

The objectives of U.S. civil space activities should be: (1) to expand knowledge of the Earth, its environment, the solar system, and the universe; (2) to create new opportunities for use of the space environment through the conduct of appropriate research and experimentation in advanced technology systems; (3) to develop space technology for space applications and, wherever appropriate, make such technology available to the commercial sector; (4) to preserve U.S. preeminence in critical aspects of space science, applications, technology, and manned space flight; (5) to establish a permanently manned presence in space; and (6) to engage in international cooperative efforts that further the United States' overall space goals.

Commercial Space Policy. The United States does not intend to preclude or deter the continuing development of a separate, nongovernmental, commercial space sector. Expanding private sector investment in space by the market-driven commercial sector generates economic benefits for the nation and supports governmental space sectors with an increasing range of space goods and services. Governmental space sectors should purchase commercially available space goods and services to the fullest extent possible and should not conduct activities with potential commercial applications that preclude or deter commercial sector space activities, except for national security or public safety reasons. Commercial sector space activities should be supervised or regulated only to the extent required by law, national security, international obligations, and public safety.

National Security Space Policy. The United States conducts those activities that it deems necessary for national defense. Space activities should contribute to national security objectives by (1) deterring, or if necessary, defending against enemy attack; (2) assuring that forces of hostile nations cannot prevent American use of space; (3) negating, if necessary, hostile space systems; and (4) enhancing operations of United States and allied forces. Consistent with treaty obligations, the national security space program should support such functions as command and control, communications, navigation, environmental monitoring, warning, surveillance, and force application (including research and development programs that support these functions).

Intersector Policies. The United States government endeavors to maintain and coordinate separate national security and civil operational space systems where differing needs of the sectors dictate. Survivability and endurance of national security space systems are to be pursued commensurate with the planned use in crisis and conflict, with the threat, and with the availability of other assets to perform the mission. Government sectors should encourage, to the maximum extent feasible, the development and use of United States private sector space capabilities.

A continuing capability to sense the Earth remotely from space is important to the achievement of American space goals. To ensure that the necessary capability exists, the U.S. government will: (a) ensure the continuity of LANDSAT-type remote sensing data; (b) discuss remote sensing issues and activities with foreign governments operating or regulating the private operation of remote sensing systems; (c) continue government research and development for future advanced remote sensing technologies; and d) encourage the development of commercial systems, which image the Earth from space, competitive with or superior to foreign-operated civil or commercial systems.

Assured access to space, sufficient to achieve all United States space goals, is a key element of American national space policy. United States space transportation systems are to provide a robust, balanced, and flexible capability with sufficient resiliency to allow continued operations despite failures in any single system. The U.S. government will continue research and development on component technologies in support of future transportation systems. The goals of United States space transportation policy are: (1) to achieve and maintain safe and reliable access to, transportation in, and return from space; (2) to exploit the unique attributes of manned and unmanned launch and recovery systems; (3) to encourage to the maximum extent feasible the development and use of United States private sector space transportation capabilities; and (4) to reduce the costs of space transportation and related services.

Communications advancements are critical to all U.S. space sectors. To ensure that necessary capabilities exist, the U.S. government will continue research and development efforts for future advanced communications technologies. The United States will consider and, as appropriate, formulate policy positions on arms control measures governing activities in space, and will conclude agreements on such measures only if they are equitable, effectively verifiable, and enhance the security of the United States and its allies.

All space sectors are to minimize the creation of space debris. Design and operations of space tests, experiments, and systems should strive to minimize or reduce accumulation of such debris consistent with mission requirements and cost effectiveness. The U.S. will also encourage other space-faring nations to adopt policies and practices aimed at debris minimization.

Space policy is constantly being reviewed by the bodies in charge of space activities. Statements by the Office of the Press Secretary of the White House are often released with announcements of new policy directives and decisions.

A statement of July 25, 1989, for example, announced that the president, acting upon the recommendation of the vice president, had approved the continuation of the National Aerospace Plane (NASP) program as a high-priority national effort to develop and demonstrate hypersonic technologies with the ultimate goal of single-stage-to-orbit.

A March 8, 1990, statement by the Press Office of the White House indicated that the president had approved the first of a series of policy decisions for the long-term Space Exploration Initiative. Acting upon the recommendation of the vice president and the National Space Council, the president had approved a program that would give early focus to technology developments and a search for new and innovative technical approaches to the Moon and Mars missions. In particular, the policy consisted of the following elements:

- the program was to include investment in high-leverage, innovative technologies with potential to make a major impact on cost, schedule, and performance;

- the program would perform mission, concept, and system analysis studies in parallel with technology development, and would include robotics science missions;

- by spurring research and development in high-technology fields, the space program would help promote American economic leadership;

- the program would require the efforts of several agencies. NASA would be the principal implementing agency. The Department of Defense and the Department of Energy would also have major roles in the conduct of technology development and concept definition. The National Space Council would coordinate the development of an implementation strategy for the Exploration Initiative by the three agencies.

On September 5, 1990, the president announced the approval of a commercial space launch policy. The Office of the Press Secretary stated that a commercial space launch industry could provide many benefits to the United States, including indirect benefits to U.S. national security.

According to that statement, the long-term goal of the United States is a free and fair market in which U.S. industry can compete. To achieve this, a set of coordinated actions is needed for dealing with international competition in launch goods and services in a manner that is consistent with U.S. nonproliferation and technology transfer objectives.

On July 24, 1991, the Office of the Press Secretary announced a national space launch strategy, which consists of four elements.

1. Ensuring that existing space launch capabilities, including support facilities, are sufficient to meet U.S. government manned and unmanned space launch needs.

2. Developing a new unmanned but man-rateable space launch system to greatly improve national launch capability with reductions in operating costs and improvements in launch system reliability, responsiveness, and mission performance.

3. Sustaining a vigorous space launch technology program to provide cost effective improvements to current launch systems, and to support development of advanced launch capabilities complementary to the new launch system.

4. Actively considering commercial space launch needs and factoring them into decisions on improvements in launch facilities and launch vehicles.

On February 13, 1992, the vice president announced a Landsat policy. Landsat is an important satellite program that provides multispectral pictures of the Earth. It supports U.S. government needs, including those related to national security and global change research, and benefits the U.S. private sector. In May 1989, President Bush directed that continuity of Landsat-type remote sensing data be maintained, and approved a series of short-term actions to implement this policy. The National Space Policy Directive of February 1992, which was developed by the National Space Council, establishes a comprehensive, long-range strategy and assigns agency responsibilities for the future. A key element of this strategy is the assignment of management and funding responsibility for the next satellite, Landsat 7, to the agencies that have the primary requirements for the data, NASA and the Department of Defense. The strategy seeks to minimize the cost of Landsat-type images for U.S. government uses, calls on agencies to eliminate unnecessary regulations governing private sector remote sensing activities, and fosters development of advanced remote sensing technologies to reduce the cost and improve the performance of future satellites.

National Aeronautics and Space Administration

NASA was established by the National Aeronautics and Space Act of 1958, as amended (42 U.S.C. 2451 et seq.). It conducts research for the solution of problems of flight within and outside the Earth's atmosphere and develops, constructs, tests, and operates aeronautical and space vehicles. It conducts activities required for the exploration of space with manned and unmanned vehicles and arranges for the most effective utilization of the scientific and engineering resources of the United States with other nations engaged in aeronautical and space activities for peaceful purposes.[4]

Planning, coordination, and control of administration programs are the responsibility of headquarters. Directors of field installations are responsible for the execution of agency programs, largely through contracts with research, development, and manufacturing enterprises. A broad range of research and development activities are conducted in field installations by government-employed scientists, engineers, and technicians to evaluate new concepts and phenomena and to maintain the competence required to manage contracts with private enterprises.

Planning, direction, and management of research and development programs are the responsibility of four program offices, all of which report to and receive guidance from headquarters. The overall planning and direction of institutional operations at the field installations and management of institutional resources are the responsibility of the appropriate institutional associate administrator under the overall guidance and direction of the administrator.

Aeronautics, Exploration, and Technology. The Office of Aeronautics, Exploration, and Technology is responsible for the conduct of programs to develop advanced technology to enable and enhance the pursuit of national objectives in aeronautics, space and transatmospherics, including the National Aerospace Plane program; to demonstrate the feasibility of this technology in ground, flight, and in-space facilities to ensure its early utilization; and to ensure the application of agency capabilities and facilities to programs of other agencies and the U.S. aerospace industry. The office is the focal point for the Space Exploration Initiative, the long-term program of robotics and human exploration that will include sending humans to the Moon early in the twenty-first century to establish a permanent outpost and conducting human missions to the planet Mars. In addition, the office is responsible for managing the Ames, Langley, and Lewis research centers.

Space Science and Applications. This office is in charge of the administration's efforts to understand the origin, evolution, and structure of the universe, the solar system, and the integrated functioning of the Earth. It conducts space application activities, such as remote sensing of the Earth, developing and understanding microgravity processes, and developing and testing advanced space communications as well as basic and applied science to facilitate human life in space. The office is also responsible for managing the Goddard Space Flight Center and the Jet Propulsion Laboratory and maintaining contacts with the Space Studies Board of the National Academy of Sciences, the Space Applications Board, and other science advisory boards and committees. The office coordinates its activities with several government agencies, foreign interests, and the private sector. Its objectives are achieved through research and development in astrophysics, life sciences, Earth sciences and applications, solar system exploration, space physics, microgravity science, and communication and information systems. The office also utilizes the space shuttle, expendable launch vehicles, automated and human-occupied spacecraft, sounding rockets, balloons, aircraft, and ground-based research to conduct its programs.

Space Flight. The Office of Space Flight (OSF) is responsible for providing the U.S. government civil space transportation and manned space-based facilities and operations in support of the NASA mission. In fulfilling its responsibilities, OSF develops, operates, and maintains manned space-based facilities and space transportation systems and services. It is also in charge of managing the Johnson Space Center, Marshall Space Flight Center, Kennedy Space Center, and John C. Stennis Space Center. The office also plans, directs, and executes the development and acquisition, testing, and operation of all elements of the space shuttle program; plans and manages execution of prelaunch, launch, flight, landing, postflight operations, and payload assignments; maintains and upgrades the design of ground and flight systems throughout the operational period; procures necessary system hardware; manages all U.S. government civil launch capabilities, including spacelab development, procurement, and operations; and develops necessary policy with other government and commercial users of the space shuttle, and coordinates all associated research.

The Office of Space Flight is also in charge of managing and directing all aspects of the space station Freedom program and accomplishing the goals established by the president. These goals include developing a permanently manned space station by the mid-1990s with the participation of other countries, and promoting scientific research, technology development, and private sector investment in space. The Johnson Space Center, the Marshall Space Flight Center, and the Lewis Research Center are responsible for developing major elements of the space station, all of which will be launched by the Kennedy Space Center. The concept of the space station Freedom program is to create a manned base, with growth to a permanent support crew of four (the crew will initially be present only during shuttle visits), and an eventual increase in station resources and crew size.

Space Operations. The Office of Space Operations is in charge of an array of functions critical to the operations of the U.S. space programs. They include spacecraft operations and control centers, ground and space communications, data acquisition and processing, flight dynamics and trajectory analyses, spacecraft tracking, and applied research and development of new technology. The space transportation system, tracking and data relay satellite system, deep space network, spaceflight tracking and data network, and several other facilities currently provide for the requirements of NASA's space missions. A global communications system links tracking sites, control centers, and data processing facilities that provide real-time data processing for mission control, orbit and attitude determination, and routine processing of telemetry data.

Field Installations

1. *Ames Research Center.* The center, which is located at Moffett Field, CA, manages a diverse program of research and technology development in support of American aeronautics and astronautics programs and maintains unique research and test facilities including wind tunnels, simulators, supercomputers, aircraft, and flight test ranges. Among the main programs are the development of aerospace vehicle concepts through synergistic application of the center's complete capabilities ranging from computation and experimentation to flight testing; research in support of human adaptation and productivity in the microgravity environment; and research and development of human/machine interfaces and levels of automation to optimize the operation of aerospace systems of the future, as well as future hypersonic vehicles and probes. The center's main program responsibilities are concentrated in computational and experimental fluid dynamics and aerodynamics; fluid and thermal physics; rotocraft, power-lift, and high-performance aircraft technology; flight simulation and research; control and guidance; aerospace human factors; automation sciences; space and life sciences; airborne sciences and applications; space biology and medicine; atmospheric and Earth sciences; and ground and flight projects in support of aeronautics and space technology. In addition to these major program responsibilities, the center provides support for military programs and major agency projects.

2. *Goddard Space Flight Center*. This facility, located in Greenbelt, MD, conducts Earth-orbital spacecraft studies, experiment development, and flight operations. It develops and operates tracking and data acquisition systems and conducts supporting mission operations. It also develops and operates Spacelab payloads, space physics research programs, Earth science and applications programs, life science programs, information systems technology, sounding rockets and sounding rocket payloads, launch vehicles, balloon experiments, planetary science experiments, and sensors for environmental monitoring and ocean dynamics.

3. *Jet Propulsion Laboratory*. This facility, which is operated under contract by the California Institute of Technology in Pasadena, develops spacecraft and space sensors and conducts mission operations and ground-based research in support of solar system exploration, Earth science and applications, Earth and ocean dynamics, space physics and astronomy, and life science and information systems technology. The laboratory is also responsible for the operation of the deep space network in support of NASA projects.

4. *Lyndon B. Johnson Space Center*. The facility, which is located in Houston, TX, is in charge of the development and operation of the space shuttle—the manned space transportation system developed for the United States by NASA. The goal behind the shuttle program is to reduce the cost of using space for commercial, scientific, and defense needs. The center is responsible for development, production, delivery, and flight operation of the orbiter vehicle (that portion of the space shuttle that is designed to take crew and experiments into space, place satellites in orbit, and retrieve malfunctioning satellites). The shuttle crew includes pilots, mission specialists, and payload specialists. Crew personnel (other than payload specialists) are recruited, selected, and trained by the center.

   The facility is also responsible for design, development, and testing of spaceflight payloads and associated systems for manned flight; for planning and conducting manned spaceflight missions; and for directing medical, engineering, and scientific experiments that are helping people understand and improve the environment. For the space station program, the Johnson Space Center is responsible for developing the main structure of the station and for several distributed systems such as data management, guidance and control, and thermal control.

5. *John F. Kennedy Space Center*. The Florida facility designs, constructs, and maintains space vehicle and ground support equipment for launch and recovery operations. The center is also responsible for prelaunch operations, launch-related operations, and payload processing for the space shuttle and expendable launch vehicle programs, as well as landing operations for the space shuttle orbiter and recovery of the reusable solid rocket booster.

6. *Langley Research Center*. The facility, located in Hampton, VA, performs research concerning the following topics: long-haul aircraft technology;

military aircraft and missile systems technology; the National Aerospace Plane; fundamental aerodynamics; computational fluids dynamics; propulsion/airframe integration; unsteady aerodynamics and aeroelasticity; hypersonic propulsion; aerospace acoustics; aerospace vehicle structures and materials; computational structural mechanics; space structures and dynamics; controls/structures interaction; interdisciplinary research; aerothermodynamics; aircraft flight management and operating procedures; advanced displays; computer science; electromagnetics; automation and robotics; reliable, fault-tolerant systems and software; aircraft flight control systems; advanced space vehicle configurations; advanced space station development; technology experiments in space; remote sensor and data acquisition and communication technology; space electronics; planetary entry technology; space power conversion and transmission; and space environmental effects and systems analysis for advanced aerospace vehicles.

7. *Lewis Research Center*. The center, located in Cleveland, OH, manages the design and development of the power generation, storage, and distribution system for space station Freedom. The center is also responsible for conducting research and technology activities in the following fields: air-breathing propulsion systems, including those needed for the National Aero-Space Plane; turbomachinery thermodynamics and aerodynamics; fuel and combustion; aero and space propulsion systems; power transmission; internal engine computational fluid dynamics; materials; structural analysis; instrumentation; controls; space electronics; cryogenics; high-temperature engine instrumentation; space communications, including design and development of the Advanced Communications Technology Satellite; design and development of microgravity flight experiments scheduled to be flown on board the space shuttle over the next few years; management of a complementary microgravity ground-based research program; and management of commercial launch services of medium-class expendable launch vehicles. In addition, the center provides research and technology support to the Department of Defense and assists the private sector in identifying potential industrial applications and commercialization of NASA-developed technology.

8. *George C. Marshall Space Flight Center*. The facility, located in Huntsville, AL, manages, develops, and tests the external tank, solid rocket booster, and main engines, which are major portions of the space shuttle project; oversees the development of the U.S. Spacelab; and conducts research in structural systems, materials science engineering, electronics, guidance, navigation, and control. For the space station Freedom program, the Marshall Space Flight Center is responsible for the pressurized laboratory and habitation modules, and the logistics module's elements supplied by the United States. The center is also responsible for systems integration of these modules.

9. *John C. Stennis Space Center*. The facility, located in Bay St. Louis, MS, plans and manages research and development activities in the field of space

and terrestrial applications; space flight; and research in oceanography, meteorology, and environmental sciences.

NASA Space Activities

As indicated above, the installations and facilities through which NASA and its other agency or private sector partners conduct space activities are numerous. Although a detailed description of those activities transcends the scope of this book, a brief summary of the main areas involved is in order.

Exploring the Universe. On May 15, 1991, the Magellan radar-mapping spacecraft completed its first "day" of studying Earth's sister planet Venus—meaning one Venus day or 243 Earth days, the time it takes the planet's surface to pass beneath the gaze of Magellan's radar.[5] The topographic map Magellan produced on its first mapping cycle is of enormous importance to space scientists, who are looking for answers as to why two very similar planets approximately the same distance from the Sun—Earth and Venus—evolved in such a different manner. Their interests go well beyond academic curiosity. Scientists feel that Magellan will contribute immensely valuable new information on the science of comparative planetology, or relating phenomena on one planet to conditions on another. Through this process, they hope to shed new light on the many factors that influence Earth's complex environment.

A matter of great interest is the "greenhouse effect" on Venus, where the extremely dense atmosphere serves to trap solar heat radiated from the surface. Unable to escape back into space, the heat has built up over time to create a surface temperature of about 900 degrees Fahrenheit. There is concern that continuing buildup of carbon dioxide in Earth's atmosphere may create a greenhouse "roof" and cause hazardous global warming. Studies of Venus's evolution may provide benefit to mankind through greater understanding of the greenhouse phenomenon.

Previous U.S. and Soviet radar-mapping spacecraft produced a good deal of general information about the surface of Venus, but their imagery lacked sufficient resolution to provide precise information about small-scale features. Magellan's advanced radar, however, has demonstrated ability to delineate sharp detail of features as small as a football field. The Venus-mapper's data offers scientists a new and vastly more detailed view of features mapped earlier, including mountains, hills, and valleys.

The Magellan program is managed for NASA by Jet Propulsion Laboratory; Martin Marietta Astronautics is the main contractor for spacecraft and Hughes Aircraft developed the radar-mapping system.

Launched on October 6, 1990, the Ulysses spacecraft is off on a voyage of discovery, breaking new scientific ground with a study of the poles of the Sun, which cannot be observed from Earth.[6] A joint project of NASA and the European Space Agency, the mission is expected to revolutionize man's knowledge of the Sun and the space around it. Ulysses carries nine instruments whose measurements will help scientists understand the major processes affecting the solar system. The 809–pound aircraft will begin its primary mission of exploring the polar regions of the Sun in June 1994. Tracking and data collection is provided by the Deep Space Network, managed for NASA by the Jet Propulsion Laboratory.

En route to Jupiter for an extensive study of the planet and its moons is the Galileo spacecraft, a cooperative U.S./German project also managed for NASA by the Jet Propulsion Laboratory. In December 1995 the Galileo main spacecraft will swing into orbit around Jupiter, imaging the planet and its moons with resolutions far better than any imagery acquired for Jupiter so far.

NASA's plans for the future include two additional solar system explorations beginning in the late 1990s and extending into the twenty-first century. The Comet Rendezvous Asteroid Flyby mission will take close looks at a comet and an asteroid on a multiyear mission. It will study the asteroid Hamburga. Then the spacecraft will rendezvous and "fly formation" with Comet Kopff, shadowing the comet for two and a half years, making high-resolution images of the comet's nucleus and studying its mineral and chemical composition. The spacecraft will also collect comet dust and samples of the comet's nucleus for on-site analysis. A companion Cassini spacecraft is being developed to fly past an asteroid in the late years of the century, make a flyby of Jupiter, then proceed to Saturn and go into orbit around the ringed planet for a comprehensive four-year study. The Jet Propulsion Laboratory is project manager for both missions with the participation of Germany and the European Space Agency.

Launched on November 18, 1989, the Cosmic Background Explorer (COBE) is studying the origins and dynamics of the universe and seeking evidence to support the Big Bang theory that the universe began with a cataclysmic explosion. Roentgen Satellite, launched June 1, 1990, is conducting a sweeping survey of x-ray sources and making dedicated observation of certain specific sources.[7] The Astro Observatory, a Shuttle-based astronomical payload designed to complement findings of the Hubble Space Telescope, is studying quasars, galaxies, and active galactic nuclei in the ultraviolet range.

NASA's space physics program seeks expanded knowledge of magnetic and electric fields, radiation, and plasmas (streams of electrified particles), and other phenomena of the Earth-Sun relationship.[8] In 1990–1991, a new satellite program called CRRES (Combined Release and Radiation Effects Satellite) provided significant advances in this area. A joint NASA/Air Force mission, the CRRES project has dual objectives: to increase scientific knowledge of the Earth's ionosphere and magnetosphere, and to gain practical benefit through monitoring the effects of the space radiation on electronic equipment. A special feature of this mission is a series of chemical-release experiments designed to aid scientists studying the processes by which fast-moving neutral gases become ionized, or electrically charged. Canisters ejected from the spacecraft release chemical vapors that visibly paint the invisible magnetic field lines with luminous particles creating, in effect, an artificial aurora. CRRES is managed for NASA by Marshall Space Flight Center and for the USAF by the Air Force Space Test and Transportation Program. The satellite was built by the Space Systems Division of Ball Corporation.

High Performance Aircraft and Future Flight. In Europe, the United Kingdom's British Aerospace and France's Aerospatiale are jointly conducting studies of a supersonic transport successor to the Concorde. Similarly, the British Rolls Royce Company and Snecma of France are working on a new engine concept for future advanced supersonic transport.[9] Japan, through its Ministry of International Trade and Industry, has started a supersonic/hypersonic technology program, initially focused on a high-speed aircraft propulsion system. These examples of investment in high-speed transport research indicate the interest of aircraft manufacturers of several nations in getting an early jump on what will be the next plateau for international aviation competition: the long-range, environmentally acceptable, and economical supersonic passenger transport. In the interest of maintaining U.S. world leadership in commercial aviation, and to tap into the economic potential of the transport market, NASA is conducting a high-speed research (HSR) program. Designed to help U.S. manufacturers prepare for the coming competition, the HSR program addresses the key technologies essential to resolving environmental and economic barriers to supersonic flight.

The HSR program follows a two-year effort that involved high-speed civil transport studies conducted for NASA by Boeing Commercial Airplane Company and Douglas Aircraft Company. The companies identified technological advances that should be possible as early as the beginning of the next century and would make supersonic flight economically competitive with the subsonic passenger airplanes of today. Of concern, however, are the environmental impact that these new concepts may have. NASA is conducting atmospheric modeling research to evaluate potential ozone depletion due to the effects of high-speed transport engine exhaust emissions. In the area of engine noise reduction, acoustic testing of model mixer-ejector nozzles demonstrated noise suppression capabilities of a degree that suggested considerable potential for achieving noise levels comparable to those required of current subsonic transports.

Materials present another research challenge. The candidate low-emission combustor concepts preclude the use of internal cooling now applied extensively, so there will be greater thermal stress on materials for the supersonic transport. This and other requirements demand material properties that cannot be met with today's technology. NASA is intensely working on a new class of ceramic-based composite materials capable of operating uncooled at 3000 degrees Fahrenheit in the combustor, and advanced high-temperature, high-strength intermetallic composites to reduce jet-exhaust nozzle structural weight.

In the field of hypersonic research, the X-30 is the focal point of joint NASA/Department of Defense National Contractor Team for the National Aero-Space Plane (NASP) program. The program is aimed at eventual development of a revolutionary class of spaceplanes capable of taking off and landing horizontally like an airplane, operating in the upper atmosphere at hypersonic speed (more than 3000 miles per hour) or flying directly into Earth orbit. Such craft would offer access to space with airplane-like flexibility and high responsiveness and a reduction in launch costs.

The National Contractor Team is a group of five major aircraft/engine firms that are sharing development costs with NASA and the DoD. The team includes three airframe companies—General Dynamics, McDonnell Douglas Corporation, and Rockwell International—and two engine manufacturers (Pratt & Whitney Division of United Technologies and Rocketdyne Division of Rockwell International).

In 1991 NASP researchers concluded the first of five planned design cycles, during which the initial working configuration of the X-30 was selected; "slush" hydrogen was selected as the propellant to reduce fuel weight, and agreement was reached on the type of propulsion system. It will be a three-segment system with three different modes of propulsion: a slow-speed module for takeoff to Mach 3, a high-speed ramjet module, and a hypersonic scramjet module. A substantial data base has been developed through ground tests of subscale engines in wind tunnels; a large-scale engine in final configuration will be tested to Mach 7 by 1993. The basic material of the X-30 airframe will be a metal composite made of high-strength silicon fibers embedded in an advanced titanium alloy.

The current stage of the NASP program involves additional design phases and complementary research in aerodynamics, aerothermodynamics, propulsion, high-temperature materials and structures, computational fluid dynamics, and other key technologies. The technical program is managed by the NASP Joint Program Office, located at Wright-Patterson Air Force Base, Dayton, OH, and staffed by Air Force, Navy, and NASA personnel. Government research facilities participating include NASA's Ames, Langley, and Lewis research centers; the USAF's Aeronautical Systems Division, Air Force Weapons Laboratory, and Arnold Engineering and Development Center; the Naval Surface Weapons Center; and the Department of Energy's Los Alamos Laboratory.

NASA's High Performance Aircraft Research program mainly explores concepts and technologies applicable to future military aircraft. Most of the activities in this field are cooperative projects with industry and agencies of the Department of Defense, such as the Air Force, Navy, and the Defense Advanced Research Projects Agency (DARPA).[10]

One current project seeks to expand the technology base for supersonic STOVL (Short Takeoff and Vertical Landing) aircraft. STOVLs are typically military tactical aircraft capable of operating from areas with limited runway space. All STOVLs in operational service are subsonic aircraft but there is interest in the United States and the United Kingdom in an advanced supersonic STOVL for future service. Since 1986 the two nations have been conducting a cooperative program aimed at developing STOVL technology; NASA and DARPA are the principal U.S. agencies involved.

NASA's work includes wind-tunnel tests of STOVL concepts and flight tests managed by Ames Research Center for the VSRA (Vertical/Short TakeOff and Landing Research Aircraft). At Lewis Research Center, NASA is conducting tests of ASTOVL propulsion systems and components. Among key research areas being explored are experimental investigations of the aircraft/ground interaction environment, propulsive lift, and flight propulsion/control integration. Propulsive lift aircraft have the capability to vary in flight the direction of the thrust generated by the propulsion system.

A related research program conducted at Ames-Dryden Research Facility involves flight testing of NASA's F-18 HARV (High Alpha Research Vehicle). The aim of NASA's High Alpha Research is to develop a design capability that will enable high-performance aircraft to achieve supermaneuverability and to maintain stability and controllability at high angles of attack. High Alpha is also being investigated in another program jointly conducted by NASA, DARPA, and the Air Force. The test vehicle is the

X-29 research aircraft, two of which were built by Grumman Aerospace Corporation to demonstrate a variety of advanced technologies that collectively offer promise of designing smaller, lighter, and more efficient military aircraft without sacrificing performance.

Integrated flight/propulsion control is being demonstrated and evaluated at Ames-Dryden in a cooperative NASA/Air Force/industry program known as HIDEC (for Highly Integrated Digital Electronic Control). In this program NASA has demonstrated that it is possible to realize significant gains in engine thrust and fuel efficiency through employment of an advanced engine control system together with engine/flight control integration. This technology could make it possible to extend the service lives of existing military aircraft and defer costly development of new types. A highlight of this program was the first demonstration of a self-repairing flight control system, one capable of identifying a component failure, isolating the failure, and reconfiguring other control elements to allow the continuance of the aircraft's mission or a safe landing.

Commercial Space Research and Development. NASA's Centers for the Commercial Development of Space (CCDS) are introducing into orbital service an innovative space system that will greatly enhance the U.S. capability for commercial experimentation in space. Known as COMET (for Commercial Experiment Transporter), the unmanned system will allow recovery of some experiment payload for analysis on Earth, and permit long-duration operation of payloads that do not need to be recovered. Boosted by an expendable launch vehicle, a "freeflyer" spacecraft will provide six cubic feet of payload volume in the nonrecoverable service module and nine cubic feet in the recoverable reentry system.[11] The freeflyer will operate in a 300-mile-high orbit for about a month, at which time the recovery system will separate for retrieval at a U.S. location, while the service module will remain in orbit to support nonrecoverable experiments for over 100 days.

System components are being designed and developed by an industry team selected after a procurement competition. Space Industries, Inc. (SII), of Webster, TX, has responsibility for recovery system development, payload integration, and orbital operations. Space Services, Inc., of Houston, TX, will provide launch services. Westinghouse Electric Company of Glen Burnie, MD, is charged with systems engineering and development of the service module. The COMET program is managed by the University of Tennessee-Calspan's Center for Advanced Space Propulsion (CASP), one of sixteen NASA-sponsored CCDS. The CCDS are competitively selected consortia of industrial firms, universities, and government organizations, established to expedite development of a technology base on which to build new commercial space industries and to assist the transition of emerging technologies from the laboratory to the marketplace.

CASP is one of seven CCDS with responsibilities in the COMET program. The Center for Advanced Materials of Columbus, OH, will provide screening and selection services for payloads developed by the CCDS and their industrial partners. Other CCDS involved in specific areas of the program are the following:

- Bioserve Space Technologies, University of Colorado (Boulder), recovery system and services;
- Center for Power, Texas A&M University, service module;
- Consortium for Materials Development in Space, University of Alabama at Huntsville, launch vehicle and services;
- Space Vacuum Epitaxy Center, University of Houston (Texas), orbital operations.

Most of the experiments carried out by NASA's CCDS are accomplished in secondary payload facilities aboard the space shuttle Orbiter. Some experiments are performed in the pressurized area of the Orbiter's middeck, where they are activated and followed by the crew. Others, known as Get Away Specials (GAS), are installed in standardized, cylindrical containers accommodated in the Orbiter's cargo bay. On Shuttle flight STS-37 the Orbiter Atlantis carried in its middeck lockers two biological space processing payloads. One, sponsored by Bioserve Space Technologies, University of Colorado, was BIMDA (Bioserve ITA Materials Apparatus), a joint development with Instrumentation Technology Associates (ITA). The payload consisted of four Materials Dispersion Apparatus (MDA) Minilab units and a Bioserve-developed Bioprocessing Testbed. The MDA is a privately financed facility designed to allow a large number of simultaneous experiments at low cost. Each MDA Minilab can accommodate as many as 150 samples for growing protein crystals and conducting biomedical and fluid science experiments. Bioserve's Bioprocessing Testbed contains hardware for six bioprocessing modules and six cell syringes.

The field of remote sensing is of enormous practical importance. The data obtained from that activity can be put to use in such applications as agricultural crop forecasting, land-use management, mineral and petroleum exploration, mapping, rangeland and forest management, water quality evaluation, disaster assessment, and many other applications. NASA's pioneering research in remote sensing technology led to commercialization of the U.S. Landsat Earth resources monitoring satellite and spawned broad expansion of airborne remote sensing. NASA is now engaged in an effort to help private industry develop and commercialize new applications of space-based and airborne remote sensing technologies.

The program, known as the Earth Observations Commercial Applications Program (EOCAP), provides government cofunding to encourage private investment in and broaden the use of NASA-developed technology for gathering and analyzing information about Earth and ocean resources. Participants include private sector organizations, educational institutions, nonprofit organizations, and government agencies. Through this program businesses are encouraged to invest, over several years, in the development and marketing of high-risk products and services useful to both the private and public sectors. Projects are selected by interested groups in response to a NASA solicitation.

Since experimenting at NASA's Centers for the Commercial Development of Space and other commercial space ventures are increasing beyond the accommodations capabilities of the shuttle Orbiter's middeck, NASA has taken a step to make additional experiment space available through a lease agreement with Spacehab, Inc., of Washington, D.C. The leased module will be carried in the Orbiter's payload bay and will add the volume equivalent of about fifty middeck lockers. The lease contract, which was signed in December 1990 and covers a five-year span through 1995, requires Spacehab, Inc., to provide the integration of the module and experiments; power, cooling, and data management; and crew training.

Pursuant to another commercial space agreement NASA is providing support to Orbital Science Corporation (OSC), of Fairfax, VA, for the company's Pegasus and Taurus commercial launch vehicles. The agreement allows OSC to enter into specific subagreements with NASA installations wherein NASA will provide, on a cost-reimbursable basis, access to the agency's launch support equipment and services. The NASA installations involved are Kennedy Space Center, Lewis Research Center, Goddard Space Flight Center, and Marshall Space Flight Center. NASA had earlier negotiated similar types of agreements with other companies— General Dynamics, LTV Corporation, Martin Marietta, and McDonnell Douglas—in the interest of fostering a strong U.S. commercial launch vehicle industry.[12]

The TIROS weather/environment satellites were developed by NASA and are now operated by the National Oceanic and Atmospheric Administration (NOAA). They obtain high-resolution images of the Earth's atmosphere for use in such applications as cloud top temperature monitoring, hazardous weather prediction, and crop monitoring. Data from the three satellites has also enabled researchers to create infrared images of the Earth's temperature; helped scientists to detect atmospheric changes such as ozone depletion, global warming, and acid rain; and has monitored the concentration of infrared-absorbing gases in the air.[13] For the real-time utilization of the satellite's information, researchers at the Center for Aerospace Sciences at the University of North Dakota, in Grand Forks, have developed a satellite tracking system. The system is designed to predict the satellite's location at any given time, enabling computer-directed pointing of ground-based antennas at the satellites' transmitters for error-free signal reception.

Predicting future satellite location is difficult. Because of the complexity of the task, University of North Dakota researchers used proven NASA satellite tracking technology computer programs known as SANTRACKS, ODG, and NORAD in developing their system. The programs were supplied to the researchers by NASA's Computer Software Management and Information Center (COSMIC) located at the University of Georgia. SANTRACKS computes the time history or groundtrack of the satellite, its field of view, and the point where the satellite is visible from a ground station. ODG allows plotting a view of Earth as seen by the satellite. NORAD makes it possible to compute sighting directions, visibility times, and the maximum elevation angle attained during each orbit.

Department of Commerce, Office of Space Commerce

The Office of Space Commerce (OSC) was established in the Office of the Deputy Secretary in 1988 with four main responsibilities:

- to act as the principal unit for coordinating space-related issues, programs, and initiatives within the department;

- to represent the department on the National Space Council at the working group level;

- to participate in international negotiations on trade in space technology;

- to encourage the export of U.S. space technology where allowed by U.S. laws and regulations; and

- to serve as an advocate for U.S. industry in interagency policy reviews and to assist industry in resolving policy questions involving the United States and foreign governments.

National Oceanic and Atmospheric Administration

The National Oceanic and Atmospheric Administration (NOAA) was formed on October 3, 1970,[14] and its mission was further defined by several other statutes, including the Land Remote Sensing Act of 1984.

NOAA's mission is to explore, map, and chart the global ocean and its living resources and to manage, use, and conserve those resources; to describe, monitor, and predict conditions in the atmosphere, ocean, Sun, and space environment; to issue warnings against impending destructive natural events; to assess the consequences of inadvertent environmental modification; and to manage and disseminate long-term environmental information.[15] Among its principal activities, the administration provides satellite observations of the environment by operating a national environmental satellite system. In addition, it conducts an integrated program of research and services relating to the oceans and inland waters, the lower and upper atmosphere, space environment, and the Earth to increase understanding of the geophysical environment. It acquires, stores, and disseminates worldwide environmental data through a system of meteorological, oceanographic, geodetic, and seismological data centers.

Department of Transportation, Office of Commercial Space Transportation

The Office of Commercial Space Transportation is the government agency responsible for regulating and promoting the U.S. commercial space transportation industry.[16] It licenses the private sector launching of space payloads on expendable launch vehicles and commercial space launch facilities. It also sets insurance requirements for the protection of persons and property and assures that space transportation activities are in compliance with U.S. domestic and foreign policy. In addition, the office is charged with promoting and facilitating the industry and provides a focal point in the federal government for formulating and implementing policies that promote the development of the American space transportation industry in the context of domestic and international competition.

Department of State

The traditional function of the Department of State has not changed significantly since the early years of the United States. The secretary of state, the principal foreign policy adviser to the president, is responsible for the overall direction, coordination, and supervision of the foreign relations of the United States and for the interdepartmental activities of the U.S. government overseas. The field of aerospace, with all its international ramifications, often involves the participation of the department in bilateral and multilateral treaties involving space activities as well as U.S. participation in international organizations and institutions that deal with space activities.

The Bureau of Oceans and International Environmental and Scientific Affairs of the Department of State has principal responsibility for the department's formulation and implementation of U.S. government policies and proposals for the scientific aspects of U.S. relations with other countries.[17] It also has management responsibility for a broad range of foreign policy issues and significant global problems related to environment, oceans, fisheries, population, nuclear technology, space, and other fields of advanced technology, and for issues of application and transfer of technology.

Among the specific functions of the bureau are the following:

- advise the secretary of state where science and technology or the bureau's functional responsibilities are concerned;
- represent the department in international negotiations in its area of responsibility;
- provide policy guidance to the U.S. oceanic, environmental, scientific, and technological communities on activities and programs affecting foreign policy issues;
- assure effective coordination of policy responsibilities between the department and the Agency for International Development in the field of science and technology; and
- direct the Environment Science and Technology Cone and the Overseas Counselor/Attaché programs.

Federal Communications Commission

The Federal Communications Commission regulates interstate and foreign communications by radio, television, wire, satellite, and cable. It is responsible for the coordinated development and operation of broadcast services and the provision of efficient national and worldwide telephone and telegraph services at reasonable rates. Its responsibilities also include the use of communications for promoting safety of life and property and for strengthening national defense.[18]

The FCC was created by the Communications Act of 1934[19] to regulate interstate and foreign communications by wire and radio in the public interest. Its regulatory jurisdiction was expanded by the provisions of the Satellite Act of 1962.[20]

The commission is composed of five members, who are appointed by the president with the advice of the Senate. One of the members is designated by the president as chairman. In carrying out its functions, the commission is assisted by a general counsel who also represents the commission before the United States Courts of Appeals; a managing director; a director of public affairs; a director of international communications; a director of legislative affairs; an inspector general; a chief engineer; a chief of plans and policy; and the chiefs of four bureaus to whom certain licensing and grant authority has been delegated.

Among the various divisions of the FCC, the Mass Media Bureau administers the regulatory program for radio, television, and direct satellite broadcasts. The bureau issues construction permits and operating licenses, and processes notifications, registrations, and petitions. The Common Carrier Communications Bureau administers the regulatory program for interstate and international common carrier communications by telephone, telegraph, radio, and satellite. Common carriers include companies, organizations, or individuals providing communications services to the public for hire, who must serve all who wish to use them at established rates.

Department of Defense and Related Agencies

U.S. government spending on space-related activities in the fiscal year 1990 totaled over $30 billion. Most of those funds are divided between NASA and the Department of Defense (DoD), with the latter getting a little over $19 billion.[21] Many are the agencies of the DoD and other organs and institutions that deal directly or indirectly with space activities. They interconnect in complex ways to provide the world's largest space defense infrastructure.

Defense Advanced Research Projects Agency. The agency is a separately organized agency within the Department of Defense under a director appointed by the secretary of defense. The agency engages in advanced basic and applied research and development projects essential to the DoD, and conducts prototype projects that embody technology that may be incorporated into joint programs or in support of selected military department programs.[22] It arranges, manages, and directs the performance of work connected with assigned advanced projects by the military departments, other government agencies, individuals, private business entities, and institutions; keeps the Undersecretary of Defense, the chairman of the Joint Chiefs of Staff, the military departments, and other DoD agencies informed on significant new developments and technological advances with assigned projects; and performs other such functions as the secretary of defense or the Undersecretary may assign.

Defense Information Systems Agency. The Defense Communications Agency, established on May 12, 1960, was renamed the Defense Information Systems Agency (DISA) by DoD Directive 5105.19 of June 25, 1991.[23] It is a combat support agency under the direction, authority, and control of the assistant secretary of defense (Command, Control, Communications, and Intelligence). Guidance for military operational policies, requirements and procedures is furnished to the agency by the chairman of the Joint Chiefs of Staff. The agency is organized into a headquarters and field activities in assigned areas of responsibility. The field organizations include the White House Communications Agency; the Joint Tactical Command, Control, and Communications Agency; and the Defense Commercial Communications Office. Among the functions of DISA are the following:

- perform systems engineering for the Defense Communications System and ensure that it is planned, operated, maintained, and managed effectively;
- provide technical and management advice and perform planning support, system engineering, and test and evaluation support through the design, development, deployment, and evolutionary phases of the Worldwide Military Command and Control System, which includes the National Military Command System and supporting communications;
- formulate the departmentwide military satellite communications architecture and define system performance criteria for the systems;
- ensure the interoperability of strategic and tactical command, control and communications and information systems used by the National Command Authority, commanders-in-chief, military departments, and agencies for joint and combined operations through the development and maintenance of joint architectures, technical interface standards, specifications, and definitions;
- provide automated information systems, analytical, and other technical support for programs managed by the chairman of the Joint Chiefs of Staff and the office of the secretary of defense;
- support national security emergency preparedness telecommunications functions of the National Communications System.

Defense Mapping Agency. Increasingly sophisticated weapon systems integral to operations of all American armed forces today simply cannot function accurately without computerized maps, charts, and operational data generated by the Defense Mapping Agency (DMA). Although millions of traditional paper maps and charts are produced annually and distributed to U.S. forces around the world, it is in the new technology of "digitization" that DMA contributes ever more significantly to military operational requirements. The almost unlimited capabilities of modern digital cartographic equipment permit DMA professionals electronically to reproduce billions of bits of information, store this data on high-density media, and transmit the information where and when needed by military commanders worldwide.

The Defense Mapping Agency was established in 1972 when the mapping, charting, and geodesy functions of the defense community were combined into this agency. It operates as a combat support agency of the DoD under the direction and authority of the assistant secretary of defense for Command, Control, Communications, and Intelligence. Among the agency's functions are the following:[24]

- enhance national security by producing and distributing timely mapping, charting, and geodetic products and services, and advising on such matters;
- provide nautical charts and marine navigational data to worldwide merchant marine and private vessel operators; and
- maintain contact with civil agencies and other national and international mapping, charting, and geodetic activities.

The mapping, charting, and geodesy functions of DMA are primarily conducted by its two major production centers. Aerospace products and support to aerospace manned and unmanned weapons systems are provided to DoD users primarily by the DMA Aerospace Center, which is located in St. Louis, MO. The DMA Hydrographic/Topographic Center is located in Brookmont, MD. A third center, the DMA Reston Center, in Virginia, was established in 1987. The center should increase the volume of mapping, charting, and geodetic products and data currently being produced by the Aerospace and Hydrographic/Topographic centers. The DMA Technical Services Center, located in Fairfax, VA, provides overall operational direction and management supervision of agency telecommunication systems and maintains and operates the long-haul systems linking major production centers and field activities.

Defense Nuclear Agency. This agency is responsible for developing nuclear weapon effects technology, expertise, and testing capabilities. The authority for its activities is included in DoD Directive 5105.31. The agency operates under the direction, authority, and control of the director, Defense Research and Engineering.[25] Agency activities are primarily focused on the development of technology to harden materials, electronics; and structures, and deploy them against blast, thermal, nuclear radiation, and other nuclear effects. The agency also advises the assistant to the Secretary of Defense (Atomic Energy) on the adequacy of military programs for the acquisition of major systems.

The agency is the focal point of the DoD for the coordination of nuclear weapons development and initial testing with the Department of Energy. In addition to other functions, it provides advice and assistance to the chairman of the Joint Chiefs of Staff and the military departments on all nuclear matters, including site security, tactics, vulnerability, radiation, and biomedical effects. The agency also provides support to the Strategic Defense Initiative Organization, particularly in the areas of lethality, survivability, and target hardening.

National Security Agency. The National Security Agency is responsible for the centralized coordination, direction, and performance of highly specialized, technical functions in support of U.S. government activities to protect U.S. communications and produce foreign intelligence information.[26] It was established by presidential directive in 1952 as a separately organized agency within the Department of Defense.

The NSA has three primary missions: an information systems security mission, an operations security training mission, and a foreign intelligence information mission. To accomplish those missions, the director of the agency has been assigned the following responsibilities:

- prescribing certain security principles, doctrines, and procedures for the U.S. government;
- organizing, operating, and managing certain activities for the production of foreign intelligence information;
- organizing and coordinating those research and engineering activities of the U.S. government that are in support of the agency's assigned functions;
- regulating certain communications in support of agency missions; and
- operating the National Computer Security Center in support of the director's role as national manager for telecommunications, security, and automated information systems security.[27]

The core of NSA's operations appears to be the collection of intelligence by means of incredibly sophisticated computers and extensive use of satellites. Signal intelligence is collected by electronic eavesdropping satellites and aircraft. Photographic intelligence is collected by reconnaissance satellites and aircraft. All signals intelligence systems are now controlled by the National Security Agency, but control over photographic and human intelligence efforts is splintered.[28] For example, another organ

in charge of overhead reconnaissance assets is the National Reconnaissance Office, the organizational structure of which is classified information. Although details on the structure of the NRO are not available to the
public, the framework may be pieced together from various sources.

Apparently, the NRO director holds the title of assistant secretary of the
Air Force for Research and Development or that of undersecretary. The
day-to-day operation of the NRO most likely falls to the director of special
projects, a directorate within the office of the secretary of the Air Force.
The head of this office doubles as deputy commander for satellite programs of the Air Force Space and Missile Systems Organization
(SAMSO), based in Los Angeles. Liaison and coordination, but not
direction, probably come through the Air Force secretary's Office of Space
Systems.[29]

According to recent news,[30] a debate is now taking place over the
possible restructuring of the intelligence apparatus of the Department of
Defense in view of recent international political developments such as the
breakup of the Soviet Union and lessons learned from the Gulf War of
1991. For example, the chief of the Central Intelligence Agency on April
1, 1992, told the members of the House and Senate Select Committees on
Intelligence that the imagery task force calls for a national imagery agency.
However, opposition from powerful bureaucratic forces, such as the
Defense Mapping Agency, may lead to a more evolutionary approach. As
part of a reorganization of the U.S. Air Force, Air Force Space Command
will take over operation of the satellite communication channels used to
relay orders to many U.S. nuclear forces around the world. The Air Force
Satellite Communications System had been operated by the Air Force
Strategic Air Command at Offutt Air Force Base, NE, which has been in
charge of U.S. nuclear bombers and Air Force nuclear missiles.[31]

Strategic Defense Initiative Organization. The Strategic Defense Initiative Organization was established as a separate agency of the Department
of Defense under the direction, authority, and control of the secretary of
defense. The agency's mission is to direct and manage the conduct of
research through advanced technology programs that will provide the
technological basis for an informed decision regarding the feasibility of
eliminating the threat posed by nuclear ballistic missiles and increasing
the contribution of defensive systems to U.S. and allied security. In the
performance of its research, the agency utilizes the services of the military
departments, the Department of Energy, private industry, and educational
and research institutions.[32]

The Strategic Defense Initiative, or "Star Wars" as it used to be called,
has been for years the subject of intense debate. When President Reagan

announced the SDI in 1983, there was a chorus of opposition claiming that a ballistic missile defense of the United States was technically impossible and, even if possible, it would cost too much. Almost ten years later, the technology has advanced, missile defenses have been tested in action, and the cost of the program has dropped significantly.

Several key elements of the SDI program are moving from research to development leading toward deployment in 1997.[33] Perhaps the most exciting technology to be proven effective is the hit-to-kill concept of missile interception. The original presidential directive was that SDI was to develop a nonnuclear defense. This made the job more difficult, since the best way to neutralize an incoming missile warhead is with a nuclear explosion. But technological advances have made it possible for interceptors to stop warheads by crashing into them, even at very high closing speeds. This was demonstrated by tests conducted high over the Pacific Ocean in 1984 and again in 1991. This incredible technology is the result of advances in on-board sensors, calibrated divert thrusters, high-speed minicomputers, and the ability to integrate other components in a functioning system. Similar advances in miniaturization have made possible innovations such as the proposed Brilliant Eyes space-based sensors and Brilliant Pebbles space-based interceptors. Ground-based defenses would back up the "Pebbles."

The SDI program proposed by the Bush administration is known as Global Protection Against Limited Strikes (GPALS) and is estimated to cost $46 billion over the next fourteen years, which is comparable to other high-tech defense programs' cost. Not excessive, some would say, considering that on the basis of present knowledge, SDI experts have little doubt that they can create a global missile-defense system.

Some of this technology was used in the Gulf War. U.S. military reconnaissance satellites deployed over the gulf were able to spot Scud rocket launchings, aiding efforts to intercept Scuds with ground-based Patriot missiles and to destroy launchers.[34] A global system would be far more sophisticated, although there has been for some time talk of international cooperation. The United States would supply and manage the space component, which could be effective against limited attack with little more than 1,000 interceptor satellites. Some military experts believe coordinating space- and ground-based defenses would be a logical role for NATO. In addition to the possible inclusion of former eastern European communist nations in NATO, NATO is also engaged in wide-ranging goodwill discussions with Russia for possible cooperation. Russian researchers have focused primarily on targeting objects in space with high-energy beams from Earth. They might be able to bring important technology to the joint defense effort.

National Science Foundation

The National Science Foundation (NSF) is an independent agency of the federal government established by the National Science Foundation Act of 1950[35] to promote and advance scientific progress in the United States. The Foundation does this primarily by sponsoring scientific and engineering research and education. NSF itself does not conduct research.

The foundation consists of a National Science Board and a director. The board is composed of twenty-four part-time members and the director ex officio. Members are appointed by the president with the advice and consent of the Senate for six-year terms. They are selected based on their accomplishments in science, medicine, engineering, agriculture, education, public affairs, research, management, or industry.

Among the most important fields that the NSF supports are the geosciences, including atmospheric sciences and mathematical and physical sciences.[36]

The atmospheric sciences program supports research to add new understanding of the behavior of the Earth's atmosphere and its interactions with the Sun. It includes:

- studies of the physics, chemistry, and dynamics of the Earth's upper and lower atmosphere and its space environment;
- research on climate processes and variations;
- studies to understand the natural global cycles of gases and particles in the Earth's atmosphere.

Specific areas of research are: aeronomy, atmospheric chemistry, climate dynamics, large-scale dynamic meteorology, magnetospheric physics, mesoscale dynamic meteorology, and physical meteorology.

The NSF also provides support to operate the National Center for Atmospheric Research (NCAR) and the Upper Atmospheric Facilities (UAF) program. NCAR scientists conduct research in atmospheric and related sciences and work with universities and other organizations to coordinate large-scale atmospheric research projects. The UAF consists of four large radar facilities located along a longitudinal chain from Greenland to Peru. They allow scientists to investigate both local and global upper atmospheric problems. The NSF also provides support for participation by U.S. scientists in international scientific research endeavors, such as the World Climate Research Program.

NSF-supported projects in the area of mathematical and physical sciences aim at developing a fundamental understanding of the physical laws that govern the universe. Research is aimed at determining the composition, structure, and evolution of planets, stars, and galaxies, including our Sun and the Milky Way. In addition to providing research grants, the National Science Foundation supports the development and operation of three national astronomy centers where radio, optical, infrared, and special telescopes are made available on a competitive basis to the scientific community. The main areas of research in the astronomical field are the following: advanced technologies and instrumentation, electromagnetic spectrum management, extragalactic astronomy and cosmology, galactic astronomy, planetary astronomy, and stellar astronomy and astrophysics.

EUROPE

The European Space Agency

A description of the European Space Agency (ESA) would technically belong in the section on international or intergovernmental organizations in that it is a supernational entity. Political developments of the last few years, however, have placed it in the same league as major national space agencies. Although several European countries still pursue their own domestic space programs in addition to their contribution to ESA, the tendency would seem to be for those space powers to merge their efforts into a larger agency—such as ESA—capable of handling the enormous budget required for space activities. In many ways, therefore, ESA is not unlike NASA or the Russian Space Agency.

In 1975 the European Space Conference, meeting in Brussels, approved the text of the convention setting up the European Space Agency. The founding members were Belgium, Denmark, France, the Federal Republic of Germany, Ireland, Italy, the Netherlands, Spain, Sweden, Switzerland, and the United Kingdom. They were joined in membership on January 1, 1987, by Austria and Norway and by Finland, which became an associate member state on the same date. In addition, Canada has an agreement for close cooperation with the agency and participates in some of its programs.

ESA was formed out of, and took over, the rights and obligations of the European Space Research Organization (ESRO) and the European Organization for the Development and Construction of Space Vehicle Launchers (ELDO).

In the words of the convention, the purpose of the Agency is: "to provide for and to promote, for exclusively peaceful purposes, cooperation among European states in space research and technology and their space applications, with a view to their being used for scientific purposes and for operational space applications systems."

In order to ensure that Europe remains at the forefront of progress,[37] one of ESA's main tasks is to prepare for its member states long-term plans proposing the direction European space research should take. ESA also plays a coordinating role by closely following the national programs of its members and, whenever possible, integrating them into its programs. A recent example of this coordinating role is the spaceplane Hermes. The initial studies for Hermes were carried out under the responsibility of CNES, the French national space center, with ESA following the progress made. At their meeting in January 1985 ESA member states' ministers expressed their interest in the program, and in 1986 the Hermes preparatory program became an ESA responsibility. The decision was made to proceed with the program at the Ministers' Conference in the Hague in November 1987.

ESA is basically an R&D organization and does not develop and manufacture its own equipment. While the definition stages of a program are the responsibility of ESA's engineers and scientists working with experts from member states, development work proper is carried out by industry under the watchful eye of ESA's staff. By placing contracts with private firms ESA ensures that Europe keeps abreast of high-technology developments and that its industry continues to play a role on the world market. Another important aspect of this system is that it tries to ensure that each member state receives money back, and has a share of the technological advances, in return for its investment in ESA. In an ideal situation, all the funds destined for industrial contracts that a member state pays into the ESA budget should return, through contracts placed by ESA, to the country of origin. In the real world, however, the system does not always work to the satisfaction of member states. The system of contractual returns has also been criticized for hindering the efficient operation of ESA and its programs.

The agency's budgets and financial operations are calculated in accounting units equivalent to the European currency unit (ECU). Exchange rates for the accounting unit vary each year and are based on the average exchange rates of the different national currencies over the first six months of the previous year. ESA's activities are either "mandatory," in which case all member states contribute to them on the basis of their average national income, or "optional," where the contributions reflect states' interest in a particular field or project. Activities carried out under the general budget and the science program are usually mandatory. Other projects, such as the European launcher, are generally optional.

The main policy making body of ESA is its council, which meets four times each year. Composed of representatives of ESA member states, the council takes decisions on the overall policy to be followed by the agency and on scientific, technical or administrative matters. For mandatory activities, each member has one vote, whereas only participating states may vote on matters relating to optional programs. The council is assisted by a number of specialized boards that oversee the management of specific ESA programs, as well as by a science program committee, an administrative and finance committee, an international relations advisory committee, and an industrial policy committee.

The agency's chief executive is the director-general, who is appointed by the council for a four-year term. He is assisted by eight directors responsible for earth observation and microgravity; science; space stations and platforms; space transportation systems; telecommunications; administration; operations; and ESTEC, as well as by his head of cabinet, the inspector-general, the associate director for policy coordination, a coordination and monitoring office, and the head of ESRIN.

The agency is headquartered in Paris; its main technical center, ESTEC—the European Space Research and Technology Center—is located in Noordwijk in the Netherlands. Its Space Operations Center, ESOC, is in Darmstadt, Federal Republic of Germany, and ESRIN, which houses the Information Retrieval Service and the Earthnet Program Office, is located near Rome, Italy. ESA's Ariane launch base is in Kourou, French Guiana. A small team of engineers are at the facilities of the French National Space Center (CNES) in Toulouse, France. In addition, ESA has a worldwide network of ground stations, including its ESTRACK station at Redu in Belgium and the observatory facilities at Villafranca in Spain, for satellite operations and a number of downrange stations for Ariane launches.

The European Space Research and Technology Center—ESTEC. In 1962 Europeans realized the need for a facility specifically designed for and devoted to the technical aspects of space research. The Netherlands were chosen as the site for this facility and the pioneers moved into rooms put at their disposal in the Technical University in Delft. By 1967 ESTEC had moved into its permanent premises at Noordwijk, some twelve miles north of the Hague on the North Sea coast. There are now more than 1,000 staff and further growth is expected. About 50 percent of the staff belong to the spacecraft project teams reporting to the program directors at ESA headquarters; most of the other 50 percent belong to specialized technical divisions that have their home base at ESTEC. These cover virtually all space disciplines and their specialized engineers are, for the most part, involved in providing support to the project teams for the technical management of ongoing projects as well as in managing the advanced R&D work that is being carried out in-house or by industry under ESA contracts.

Among the most important achievements of ESTEC are the ECS and Marecs series of communications spacecraft and, in the scientific field, Giotto, which successfully flew by Halley's Comet. Another program in which ESTEC played a leading role was Spacelab, Europe's first step in the manned space field. The next step is Columbus, the European contribution to the international space station. The Space Technology Program is one of ESTEC's key activities and it has two main goals: to ensure that the technology required by future space projects will be available on time and to stimulate Europe's competitiveness in the high-technology world market. The program is divided into three parts: the Basic Technology Program, which generates the new technology needed for future missions; the Supporting Technology Program, which continues the process and demonstrates the flight-worthiness of the systems; and the Technology Demonstration Program, which will provide in-orbit demonstration opportunities.

The European Space Operations Center—ESOC. ESOC was established at Darmstadt in the Federal Republic of Germany in September 1967 and became fully operational by May 1968. It is responsible for the operation of spacecraft in orbit, which also involves a variety of tasks carried out before and after launch. Prior to launch, ESOC specialists analyze the mission requirements so as to determine the spacecraft's orbit. After launch, their responsibilities include the tracking and control of the spacecraft as well as the reception, processing, and distribution of both spacecraft and payload data.

The center of activities, once a spacecraft has separated from its launcher, is the Operations Control Center (OCC). The OCC is permanently linked, through the ESOC communications network, with the entire network of ESA ground stations—known as ESTRACK—located around the world. During the first few weeks of a spacecraft's orbit, the main control room is used to carry out all the operations and maneuvers needed to ensure it reaches its final orbit. Once there, operational responsibility is handed over to a dedicated control room for the routine operational phase.

The ESTRACK network is an essential part of the Operations Control Center. Each station in the network is equipped both to receive spacecraft telemetry transmissions and to transmit commands and signals up to the spacecraft. The choice of the location of the stations ensures that there is sufficient overlap of ground coverage during the critical transfer and drift-orbit activities, thus avoiding any risk of endangering a mission in case of a ground station failure. Another vital element of the OCC is the central computer facility, the Multi-Satellite Support System. Not only is it used during the launch and early-orbit phases but it also supports the routine phases of those missions that do not require their own dedicated computer facilities.

ESRIN. The facility's name was given by the now-disbanded European Space Research Institute. ESRIN's function is related to information, especially information from computer-based data. Three separate divisions handle millions of pieces of information destined for ESA and outside customers.

The ESA Information Retrieval Service (ESA-IRS) is one of Europe's leading scientific and technical information sources. From its beginning, when its main task was to give the European aerospace community access to the NASA database, it has grown along with the demands of its customers. ESA-IRS has more than 130 databases and databanks accessible through the ESRIN computer with nearly 50 million items, mostly bibliographic references. In addition to traditional space sciences and technology, new space disciplines in life and materials sciences and a broad range of management information is now available for those involved in aerospace activities. To handle all this information ESA-IRS has its own software and retrieval language, ESA-QUEST, with many sophisticated methods of searching for information. Almost any part of the world is within reach of ESA-IRS's information using PCs and other terminals. Most ESA member states have a national center that acts on behalf of ESA-IRS and facilitates service.

ESA has been working towards a European remote sensing satellite system for several years. In 1978, during the early stages of this program, it was decided to set up the Earthnet Program Office (EPO) at ESRIN. Earthnet provides Europe with a center for the acquisition, preprocessing, archiving, and distribution of remote sensing data. Earthnet operates through a network of receiving stations located in the far north of Sweden, in Norway, in Italy, and in the Canary Islands. Spacecraft data, in digital form, are received by any of these stations and processed into machine-readable form. Users can be provided with various types of information including photographic images.

ESA and its industrial partners are continuously generating data. To support control and automation of the data and to prepare for the highly complex information flows that will be part of the new major programs Columbus, Hermes, and Ariane 5, the agency has set up a new division at ESRIN—the Information Systems Division. This new division is responsible for a number of new activities, including the European Space Information System, the ESA Documentation Service, and the Information Technology Office.

Among the main activities conducted or sponsored by ESA are: Earth Observation, the Telecommunications Program, Space Transportation Systems, and Space Station.

Earth Observation. ESA's Earth Observation Program covers two main fields. One is the observation of the seas, oceans, and land masses. The other is observation of the atmosphere, which provides meteorological information. Also included in the program is what is known as a solid earth project; that is, a mission designed to improve our understanding of the physical forces and processes active below the Earth's surface that are responsible for volcanic eruptions and earthquakes.

The Telecommunications Program. ESA has built its telecommunications program in a series of logical steps. After a first preoperational satellite, OTS, launched in 1978, it has set up two first-generation operational systems. Its European Communication Satellite System spacecraft, which now form part of the Eutelsat space segment, meet the requirements of both the European PTT administrations for international telephone traffic in Europe and of the European Broadcasting Union for its television exchange network, Eurovision. The second step was the Maritime ECS spacecraft. The third step is Columbus, a large multi-purpose telecommunications spacecraft. For the future, ESA already has its eyes set on new data relay satellite systems for the space station (DRS) to ensure a continuous flow of data to and from the station and a central point on the ground.

Space Transportation Systems. In 1973 ESA member states approved the development of a European launcher to give Europe an independent launch capability for its own satellites, and to enable Europe to acquire a share of the international satellite launch market.

The development of the Ariane launcher is an excellent example of European cooperation at the industrial level: some forty aerospace firms throughout Europe are involved in the development and manufacturing of Ariane. Manufacturing of units and their launches are handled by Arianspace, a private company set up to take over operational responsibility from ESA. The Ariane launch base is situated near the town of Kourou in French Guiana, just over five degrees north of the equator. This location offers a tremendous advantage, particularly for the launch of geostationary satellites. Because the launch base is an uninhabited area near the Atlantic coast, spacecraft can be launched in any direction from due north through an angle of more than 90° to the east without posing any risks to people or property.

Hermes, the messenger of the gods, is the name of Europe's spaceplane, which was originally designed to carry crew and payload elements to and from the space station. Its mission has been somewhat scaled down to exclude the crew but remains a formidable challenge in the years ahead. It will call for the development of new technology in many fields and will undoubtedly help to boost the European aerospace industry into the twenty-first century.

Space Station. The successful first flight of Spacelab in 1983 represented an important milestone on the road toward European manned space flight. This flight represented the culmination of many years' effort to meet the challenge of developing an in-orbit laboratory. In 1984 the president of the United States invited friends and allies to join with his country in creating a permanent presence in space. That invitation received an enthusiastic response not only from Europe but from Canada and Japan as well. The international space station, now known as space station Freedom, represents one of the greatest technological, financial, and political challenges yet encountered in the peaceful exploration and exploitation of space. ESA will contribute to the venture through its Columbus Development Program.

The Columbus Development Program includes the development, manufacturing and delivery to orbit of three elements: a laboratory attached to the station core, a free-flying laboratory, and an independent platform. The program also includes the build-up of the related ground infrastructure. The Columbus attached laboratory is a pressurized cylindrical module that will be permanently attached to the manned base of space station Freedom. It will be used primarily for payloads and experiments in materials science, fluid physics, and life sciences requiring the permanent presence of people. The module will be launched and serviced by the space shuttle. The Columbus free-flying laboratory will consist of a two-segment pressurized module for the accommodation of payloads and an unpressurized resource module to provide the necessary power, data handling, and life-support systems. The Columbus platform is an unmanned platform designed to operate in a highly inclined Sun-synchronous polar orbit. It will be used primarily for Earth observation missions and will be operated in conjunction with other platforms provided by the international partners.

The Science Program. ESA's Science Program is the main element of the agency's mandatory activities in which all ESA members participate and is a driving force behind many other activities. Nineteen eighty-five was an important milestone in the history of ESA's Science Program. It saw the approval of a long-term plan for scientific research in space (Horizon 2000), designed to ensure that Europe continued to play a key role in this field through the early years of the next century and beyond. The program is built around the following four major missions to be carried out during the next twenty years:

- the *Solar-Terrestrial Physics Program*, which will build on the extensive experience gained in Europe over the past twenty-five years in solar, heliospheric, and space plasma physics. Soho (for Solar and Heliospheric Observatory) and Cluster jointly make up this mission;

- an *X-ray Observatory* mission for the study of large- and small-scale structures of the hot components of the matter in the universe;

- a *Planetary Science Mission*, which would consist of bringing back to Earth samples of materials from asteroids and comets;

- a *Second Astronomy Mission*, concentrating on very high-resolution spectroscopy of the submillimiter wave length domain, to study the physical processes at work in the cool matter of the universe.

In addition to the four major projects above, a number of medium-size and small projects are also under way or planned. Among the medium-size projects are Ulysses and the Hubble Space Telescope. Ulysses's mission is to explore the third dimension of the solar system by flying high over the poles of the Sun. The Hubble Space Telescope, which is being developed by NASA with substantial ESA particiation, is expected to revolutionize the study of astronomy over the next decade or so.

As a result of more than twenty years of the coordinated European effort in the space field, a space sector has emerged in an industry that has been growing steadily and has given Europe a significant role in the competitive high-technology market. In addition to the production of scientific or applications spacecraft, launchers, ground control systems, and related equipment, there has been a development of other sectors of industry that can properly be described as a spinoff of space R&D.

With most private companies having acquired a solid experience of collaboration at an international level, the European space industry has now reached a high degree of maturity. This is well illustrated by its presence on the international telecommunications market, where it is involved in programs for organizations such as Intelsat, Eutelsat, Inmarsat, and Arabsat, or other operational fields such as meteorology. By managing so many programs, ESA's staff have acquired an invaluable capital of technical know-how that is recognized and appreciated by industry.

Austria

The main Austrian institution dealing with space activities is the Austrian Space Agency (ASA). According to its Terms of Reference, it has the following tasks:

- To coordinate projects in the field of space research and technology in Austria and abroad, as well as within the framework of international organizations;
- to establish and maintain contacts with foreign institutions engaged in space research and technology;
- to advise the Austrian government on matters concerning space research and technology in line with Austrian interests and requirements and taking into account international developments in this field;
- to process information and data on space research and to distribute them to all interested parties in Austria, as well as to publish relevant documents;
- to promote the training of specialists in the field of space, in cooperation with university institutes and research organizations within Austria and abroad;
- to carry out public relations activities, in particular organization of relevant meetings;
- to promote the awarding of contracts to industry and scientific institutions in Austria;
- to act as secretariat to the "Advisory Committee on Space Research and Technology" of the Austrian federal government.

All these activities must be carried out without ASA-owned research facilities. It is ASA's task to support and promote the activities of existing scientific and industrial institutions in the field of space research and technology.

On January 1, 1987, Austria became a full member of the European Space Agency (ESA). One of the most important functions of the Austrian Space Agency is to coordinate Austria's participation in ESA. In particular, it must safeguard the interests of Austrian industry by securing industrial returns and to assist in the obtaining of industrial contracts. ASA staff members have acted as delegates or consultants in a number of bodies of ESA such as the council, and the Science Program Committee, as well as relevant program boards.

In 1990 the Federal Ministry for Science and Research, the Federal Ministry for Public Economy and Traffic, the Federal Economic Chamber, and ASA all collaborated in the elaboration of a concept for a national space technology development program, based on proposals from interested Austrian firms and research institutions. The purpose of the Austrian National Space Technology Program (ANSTP) is basically to support Austrian industry by enabling Austrian private companies to become more competitive.

ASA is a member of the Consultative Commission for Space Research and Technology and also acts as its secretary. During 1989–1990 members of the commission were representatives of the Federal Ministry for Science and Research, the Federal Ministry for Foreign Affairs, the Federal Ministry for Public Economy, and Traffic and the Federal Ministry for Finance, as well as the Conference of Rectors, the Austrian Academy of Sciences, the Federal Economic Chamber, the Fund for the Promotion of Scientific Research, the Fund for the Promotion of Research for Commerce, the Austrian Labor Board, The Austrian Federal Trade Union, the Union of Austrian Industrialists, the Austrian Industry Agency, and the Institute for Economic Research. The commission has the following tasks:

- to elaborate a long-term strategy for Austria's participation in space projects;
- to make recommendations on whether Austria should participate on specific optional ESA programs;
- to make recommendations on the use of financial resources (both within Austria and with regard to ESA) and to examine whether they are used in accordance with the original purpose;
- to advise the government on the nomination of delegates to ESA;
- to coordinate space activities within Austria, taking into account international developments.

ASA and twelve other Austrian institutions are members of the European Association of Remote Sensing Laboratories (EARSeL). The objective of the association is to promote remote sensing activities in Europe and to provide a forum for an exchange of ideas among scientists.

As of 1989 an ASA staff member also represents Austria in the Space Frequency Coordination Group (SFCG). The objective of the group is to coordinate the distribution of frequencies for space projects and to pass on the relevant information to the respective national postal administrations, so that their requirements can be taken into account at the planning conferences that are held regularly.

Basic agreements without any financial obligations were concluded with NASA and with the space agencies of France, Germany, Norway, Sweden and Switzerland and serve as a basis for co-operative projects. The financial requirements of these bilateral projects are not met by ASA's budget, but must be provided by the Austrian institutions concerned. Efforts have also been made to initiate cooperation among Spanish, Italian, and Austrian industrial and research institutions.[38]

Belgium

Belgium has been a member of the European Space Agency since its inception and most of its space programs are undertaken within or under the auspices of ESA. Its participation in the European space success has been substantial. Thanks to Belgium's membership in ESA, Belgian manufacturers and scientists can participate in programs on an international scale, the magnitude of which offers challenges far greater than would be possible on a national level.

In 1988 the Institutional Reform Act reorganized the allocation of responsibilities among the state, communities, and regions. The minister for science policy and the secretary of state for science policy are to stimulate and coordinate the development of science and technology at the national government level.[39] Operating under the aegis of the minister for science policy and the secretary of state for science policy, the Science Policy Office (SPO) is responsible for developing the broad lines of national science policy and undertaking a number of tasks in the following areas:

- management of the interuniversity networks for fundamental research and national research programs funded by the Ministry for Science Policy;
- participating in international activities and programs for scientific and technological cooperation, and funding research projects conducted by Belgium within the framework of various international organizations;
- preparing the interdepartmental science policy budget program and cooperation between government departments with regard to international scientific cooperation.

Other institutions responsible for space-related activities are: the National Committee for Space Research (CNRS) and its subcommittees, the Royal Meteorological Institute, the Royal Belgian Observatory, the Astrophysics Institute of Liege University, and the Belgian Institute of Space Aeronomy.

Remote sensing ranks among the space fields that most interest the Belgian government. The research and development program in that sector, which has been named Telsat, studies the scientific and socioeconomic implications of data obtained from the American LANDSAT satellites, the French SPOT, and the European ERS. The Scientific Policy Planning Services (SPPS) started a program in 1984 to coordinate the efforts of universities and laboratories in the study of remote sensing applications in the field of geography and natural resources.

The first stage of the remote sensing program produced the following results:

- the development of appropriate scientific methods to utilize satellite data concerning the Earth's surface;
- the training of experts in the various fields of remote sensing;
- the participation of Belgian scientists in European programs and the utilization of Belgian know-how in remote sensing.

The success of the first program led SPPS to subsidize another program, called Telsat II, which is to include studies in the fields of geology, atmospheric research, and instrument development. In the fields already financed during the first stage, such as agriculture and land management, emphasis is placed on the refinement of techniques in the hope that they will become an instrument of environment management. The Belgian Telsat research has been carried out also at an international level within ESA, the European Economic Community, and in cooperation with international organizations such as UNESCO and the World Wildlife Foundation (WWF).

The SPOT Program, in cooperation with France and Sweden, concerns the development of remote sensing satellites with optical sensors for the reception and processing of images. Belgium has contributed 4 percent of the cost of developing SPOT 1 and 2 and 1 percent for SPOT 3 and 4, which will be launched in 1995.

The MIRAS Program with the Moscow Institute for Cosmic Research concerns the utilization of the Mir space station with a spectrometer developed by the Belgian Institute of Space Aeronomy and built by the company ETCA.

The Global Change Program attempts to mobilize the world to monitor the environment on a global scale. In that context, the Belgian government established at the end of 1990 a national program for a four-year period. The objectives of that program are: an improved understanding of the interactions among physical, chemical, and biological processes and how they affect the global ecosystem; the elaboration of techniques to prevent undesirable changes; and the study of human activities and their effects on climate variations.

Another field of Belgian involvement in space activities is that of telecommunications. The RTT (Telephone and Telegraph Administration) is responsible for all telecommunications in Belgium, including those utilizing satellites. RTT represents Belgium in international organizations relating to satellites such as INTELSAT, INMARSAT, and EUTELSAT. Among the telecommunications facilities in Belgium are the following:

- The Liedekerke Geostation became operational on February 25, 1985, and provides television links within the EUTELSAT system. The Liedekerke stations 2 and 3 became operational in December 1987 and provide digital links for private use. They work with the Intelsat Business Services and cover the business needs of private companies that have small downlinks on their premises.

- The RTT Station at Lessive, near Rochefort, was inaugurated in September 1972 and has continued to grow since then. It connects the RTT network with both INTELSAT and EUTELSAT.

- The ESA Station at Redu was established in 1968 by the European space community for the study of telemetry and scientific satellites. It has acquired a new dimension with the operation of satellites for telecommunications and meteorology. The facility has become the control center for ECS satellites on the geostationary orbit in the Eutelsat system. It is now also equipped for communication with the Olympus satellite and has been chosen for the control and orbit tests of the next European telecommunications satellite. The facility is managed for ESA by CISET International.

Among other space activities in which Belgium participates are:

- *Ariane.* Thanks to the growing market for scientific, telecommunications, meteorological, direct TV, and Earth-observation satellites, the development of a range of reliable and competitive launchers by the European Space Agency is beginning to achieve commercial success. Since 1979 some forty satellites have been launched at the Kourou Space Center in French Guiana, two-thirds on behalf of Arianspace, the first commercial transportation company. Belgium has made a 5 percent contribution to the costs of the Ariane rocket development programs (6 percent for Ariane 5). As a result, several Belgian firms are now actively involved in commercial space projects.

- *Spacelab-Eureca.* Like Ariane, Spacelab is one of the great European achievements in space. The Spacelab crew consists of American and European scientists and engineers. The laboratory can accommodate up to four people. The first Spacelab flight was a manned flight in 1983, and of the seventy-seven experiments carried out, sixty-one were European, with the Belgian experiments being conducted on behalf of the Belgian Institute of Space Aeronomy, the Royal Meteorological Institute, Antwerp University, and the Catholic University of Louvain. On its third flight, in 1985, the Belgian experiments were concerned with fluid physics and the manufacture of composite materials.

- *Space Transport and Space Station.* Europe is determined to acquire a full independent space capability. This calls for space transport capability and the development of a permanent space station. ESA member states have decided to respond to the U.S. proposal to participate in the development and utilization of the future international space station. This program, called Columbus, has a 5 percent Belgian participation. A substantial financial effort to make a permanent space infrastructure available is warranted only if Europe has the facilities to link it with the ground by means of flights for regular maintenance and supplies. The space transport vehicle, comparable to the proposed U.S. National Space Plane (NASP), is being prepared by ESA and will be called HERMES. To this program, which has recently been somewhat scaled down, Belgium is making a 5.8 percent contribution. Training of the Hermes astronauts, if there will be any, will be partly done at the Pilot Training Facility in Belgium.

France

France is one of the countries at the helm of the European space effort. Both its national space programs and its contribution to the European Space Agency and other international programs place it on the cutting edge of European space technology.

The Centre National d'Etudes Spatiales (CNES), a government body, commercial and industrial in character, is the national agency responsible for the development of French space activities. Created in December 1961, CNES began operations on March 1, 1962. Its main mission is to:

- analyze the long-term issues and future course of space activities and to submit proposals to the French government regarding the programs and facilities required to enable France and Europe to participate in their development; and
- conduct the major development programs undertaken as a national effort as well as certain activities within ESA in pursuance of the French government's space policy decisions.[40]

In discharging its mission, CNES plays several roles:

- in association with the scientific community, it implements a fundamental research program in the space field, involving the laboratories of the Centre National de la Recherche Scientifique (CNRS) and France's universities;

- it develops supplier-customer–type relationships with French users of space such as France Telecom, the Broadcasting Authority (Télédiffusion de France), the Ministry of Defense, the Meteorological Office, and Earth-observation users;
- it strives to foster the competence of French exporting firms by awarding them, whenever possible, project contracts and responsibility for their execution;
- in the operations area, CNES plays an important role by providing services for satellite control and operation of the Kourou launch range;
- it strives to capitalize on the technical know-how acquired through space programs by initiating the establishment of marketing companies whenever the space applications market warrants it and there are no structures yet to take on such activities;
- in association with the Ministry of Foreign Affairs, CNES represents France on the various bodies of the European Space Agency.

As of 1991, the staff level of CNES stood at over 2,400, working at one of the following locations: CNES headquarters in Paris; the Launcher Division in Evry; the Toulouse Space Center (CST)—program preparation and development, exploitation of operational systems, heavy test facilities, and the Hermes directorate; and the Guaiana Space Center (CSG), a launch range located in French Guyana.

The activities of CNES include French participation in ESA's programs as well as cooperative national and international programs. National programs include research and technology activities; the SPOT program in Earth observation (with Belgian and Swedish participation), which led to the establishment of the world's first commercial satellite remote sensing system in 1986; and the deployment, in cooperation with other government bodies, of the Telecom 1 system, followed by the Telecom 2 system and the future military observation satellite, Helios. Bilateral cooperation includes scientific projects with the United States and the former Soviet Union; direct broadcasting, with the Franco-German TDF/TV-SAT program; and location and data collection with the Argos program, carried out in cooperation with the United States. With respect to participation in ESA's programs, CNES has been a driving force in the adoption and conduct of the ARIANE project. It also originated the Hermes spaceplane project.

It is imperative for CNES to maintain and develop the know-how and skills of both industry and the scientific community in order to foster France's space effort. This goal is pursued through various forms of cooperation with the existing industrial community and, where necessary, by the creation of new commercial ventures. CNES currently holds shares in eight companies and participates in four consortia. Its activities span a large range of sectors:

- space transportation, with ARIANESPACE,
- Earth observation, with SPOT IMAGE and SSC SATELLIT BILD,
- providing consulting and training for remote sensing, through SCOT CONSEIL and the GDTA,
- space communications, with SATEL CONSEIL,
- position-location, with CLS ARGOS,
- funding and promoting space technology, with NOVESPACE and PROSPACE,
- space activity support, through INTESPACE, MEDES/IMPS, and SIMKO.

In addition to these commercially oriented activities, CNES is also a member of more scientifically oriented consortia. They include: ULTRA-SONS, a medical research organization; CCVR and CERFACS, two groups devoted to scientific computation research; and OST, an entity that tracks, collects, and compiles science and technology indicators.

ARIANSPACE. In March 1980, thirty-six manufacturers and thirteen banks from eleven different European countries combined with the French space agency CNES to create ARIANSPACE SA—the first commercial space transportation company in the world. Ten years later, on February 1, 1990, the founding members created a holding company, ARIANSPACE Participation, which opened the capital of the company to a number of additional European partners.

ARIANSPACE SA is responsible for the funding, marketing, production, management, and operation of the Ariane 4 launcher. A subsidiary, S3R, provides launch risk insurance for ARIANSPACE customers. The company has already captured over half of the world's commercial satellite launch market and is actively preparing for the future, in particular the upcoming entry into service of the next-generation Ariane 5.

CNES and ESA defined the French agency's mission and responsibilities in regard to ARIANSPACE. Throughout the operational phase, CNES's launcher division (DLA) is responsible for launch vehicle qualification, as well as the associated ground facilities and operating system. In addition, as design authority, the launcher division provides ARIANSPACE with technical support and also supplies quality assurance services.

CLS ARGOS. CLS (Collecte et Localisation par Satellite) was established in 1986 to process, distribute, and market raw data and value-added products generated by various satellite-based data collection and location systems. CLS provides consulting, training, and engineering services. CLS is a private sector subsidiary of CNES, IFREMER (French Institute of Marine Research). It is headquartered in Toulouse, where its main development center is also located. It has eighty employees, mostly engineers and technicians, with experience in space and information technologies. The company pursues a growth strategy that focuses on three areas:

1. Development of the company's computing tools, centered not only in Toulouse but also in Landover, Maryland, and other regional centers such as those in Australia and Japan. The goal is to create a global network of technical expertise that matches global satellite coverage, and thus enables the processing and distribution of data anywhere in the world.

2. The company has also signed licensing agreements and works in cooperation with major satellite system operators. CLS operates the following systems under license:

   - ARGOS, a system under the control of CNES and the National Oceanic and Atmospheric Administration (NOAA) of the U.S., makes use of satellites in low Earth orbit to help monitor our planet and protect the environment.

   - The Meteosat data collection system, which provides access to data collection via geostationary satellites, under the control of EUMETSAT (European Meteorological Satellite Organization).

   - DORIS, a CNES-led system, provides very high precision orbitography for the satellites on which it is installed, and also offers a worldwide, extremely accurate position-locator system with operational characteristics very similar to those of ARGOS.

3. CLS is diversifying its technological capabilities in two ways:

   - the creation of a space oceanography group, whose activities are focused on satellite-based elevation data;

   - by working closely with CNES in order to participate in the preparation of space systems scheduled to enter into service around the turn of the century.

GDTA. The Groupement pour le Développement de la Télédetection Aérospatiale (GDTA) was set up in July 1973 by the CNES and the Institut Géographique National (IGN). Later, the two founding members were joined by the Institut Français du Petrole, the Bureau de Recherches

Geologiques et Minieres, the Bureau pour le Developpement de la Production Agricole, and the Institut Français de Recherche pour l'Exploitation de la Mer. All six members are government organizations.

The GDTA's main goal is to promote remote sensing and develop the use of satellite imagery. Among its functions are the following:

- to provide remote sensing training courses at both introductory and advanced levels for professionals working in areas likely to benefit from remote sensing technology, including cartography, geology, agriculture, urban planning, oceanography, and geographic information systems;

- to organize technology transfers to foreign countries by organizing seminars and training courses and by seconding experts under the auspices of the French Ministry for Cooperation, the French Ministry for Foreign Affairs, or international institutions. The GDTA helps set up training development programs for remote sensing centers. An example of these projects are those undertaken in Nairobi, Kenya, and Bangkok, Thailand;

- to distribute satellite imagery (except SPOT). The GDTA is the supplier of Landsat data in France and other countries as a representative of Eurimage (Italy) and Eosat (USA). GDTA also distributes NOAA data and experimental space programs data;

- to organize and conduct airborne operations to test new sensors as part of satellite-borne instrument development programs.

INTESPACE. This center was founded in 1983 to provide engineering expertise in space environment testing. Created as a CNES subsidiary, it took over the operations of a Toulouse-based company, Sopemea. The shareholders of INTESPACE are the following: CNES, 35 percent; Sopemea, 35 percent; Matra, 9 percent; Aerospatiale, 9 percent; Alcatel Espace, 3 percent; and Mutual Fund, 9 percent. The total staff of 160 includes fifty engineering and management staff and eighty technicians.

INTESPACE is one of the few European test centers equipped to prepare, carry out, and interpret the results of environmental tests on spacecraft. The company has also diversified its activities to include aviation, defense, and other industries. The main facilities in Toulouse include:

- satellite assembly and integration halls adjacent to the test facilities;
- electrodynamic shakers;
- a space environment simulation chamber with a 3.8-meter diameter solar simulator;
- a thermal vacuum-test chamber, ten meters in diameter;
- a reverberation chamber with a maximum level of 156 dB.

Many space programs have used INTESPACE's test facilities, including French satellites Telecom 1 and Spot, the European satellites Immersat and Italsat, and scientific missions such as Vega, Spacelab, and Sigma. INTESPACE also places its technical expertise at the service of customers needing environmental studies and provides engineering services for test centers outside of France.

MEDES/IMPS. The word MEDES is the contraction of the French words Medecine and Espace; IMPS stands for the Institut de Medecine et Physiologie Spatiales. MEDES/IMPS was set up in late 1989 in response to a new demand for expertise in space life sciences. At the time, demand was rising as work began on Europe's Hermes and Columbus manned programs. French laboratories with expertise on the subject had contributed significantly to space physiology and biology experiments conducted during flights by French astronauts on board the Soviet Salyut and Mir space stations and French astronaut flights on the U.S. shuttle. All the laboratories had received CNES certification for participation in space programs.

MEDES/IMPS is a joint venture set up on the initiative of CNES. The three main members are CNES, the Toulouse main hospital, and the regional sports education organization. A number of teams and laboratories known for their work in gravitational physiology are also members. CEA, the French atomic energy commission, contributes important experience in the field of radiation protection. In setting up MEDES, CNES united under a single masthead all major sources of French know-how in space physiology and medicine, which until then had been widely scattered.

MEDES provides a range of services to national space agencies, ESA, and industrial firms in the field of manned space flight. In particular, MEDES organizes and participates in on-board operations on behalf of space agencies. This work covers the selection, preparation, and training of crew members before flights, medical and psychological support and preventive measures during flights, and long-term follow-up after flights.

NOVESPACE. CNES created its NOVESPACE subsidiary in 1986, and has a 48 percent stake in the company. The main objective of NOVESPACE is to transfer technology by selling inventions and new technologies on a commission basis. The field of specialty for this company is microgravity, where it enjoys a virtual monopoly in the French market. It is also developing other means of access to microgravity technology using retrievable capsules.

PROSPACE. The French space industry association was founded in 1974, following an initiative by CNES to help domestic space industry promote business and export products and expertise. Today, PROSPACE has over fifty space-related companies and organizations, ranging from prime contractors and equipment developers and component manufacturers to test centers and financial institutions.

SATEL CONSEIL. Founded in 1978 by CNES, TDF (Télédiffusion de France) and FCR (France Cables and Radio), the SATEL CONSEIL consortium has the basic function of providing international consulting, engineering, and technical assistance services in the field of space communications. It offers its customers access to France's extensive space communications experience as well as its human and material resources. Through SATEL CONSEIL, customers can also take advantage of the wide-ranging expertise and resources of CNES, TDF, and France Telecom (through FCR), as well as the research and development centers, such as CNET telecoms research center, Mobiles Division, and DTRE international telecoms operator.

SATEL CONSEIL has carried out a number of satcom system feasibility studies for numerous countries or groups of countries. It has also been involved in several definition studies for systems such as Arabsat (second generation), Eutelsat II, Koreasat, Palapa C., Rascom, and Simon Bolivar. Certain contracts—notably those concerning international organizations such as Aseta, ESA, Eutelsat, Inmarsat, and Intelsat—were performed within the framework of the European Satellite Consulting Organization (ESCO), a consortium that groups SATEL CONSEIL, Detecon (Germany), and Telespazio (Italy).

SCOT CONSEIL. In September 1987, SCOT CONSEIL was formally established as a subsidiary of CNES. The company's basic function is to provide services, including engineering consultancy, advice, and technical support in connection with systems devoted to satellite-based Earth observation. SCOT CONSEIL is also involved in project coordination, both during the preparatory and execution phases, in the promotion of and in making better known remote sensing generally, particularly among major international organizations active in development funding. Among the areas of SCOT CONSEIL's expertise are remote sensing and Geographic Information Systems (GIS).

SPOT IMAGE. This is a French company set up on July 1, 1982, to distribute—worldwide and on a nondiscriminatory basis—geographical information gathered by the Spot Earth observation system. To promote the Spot system, SPOT IMAGE has set up a network of over fifty distributors around the world. Spot satellites transmit image data to direct receiving stations, of which there are currently fourteen. Two of these, located at Kiruna (Sweden) and Toulouse (France), also receive image data stored in on-board recorders, giving access to any region in the world.

The SPOT IMAGE catalog already contains entries on over 2 million images available from archives. The computerized databank is updated and accessible around the clock. Access was even upgraded recently with the commissioning of the DALI (Device to Access and Look at Spot Imagery) system. DALI enables users to view any image of interest directly on their computer, along with all relevant technical information.

Defense-related Issues. According to recent news reports,[41] the French government has begun a wide-ranging research effort to couple its military space ambition with its already well-established civilian space program. The primary goal of the research would be to narrow the gap between the current American military space capability and the relatively undeveloped space defense capability of France and Europe. French government and industry officials say that their goal is to have, by early in the next decade, a full range of radar, optical, and electronic surveillance satellites linked by data-relay spacecraft. In order to maximize the return on the large investment involved, the French arms procurement agency, Délégation Générale pour l'Armement (DGA), is working in tandem with the CNES on a host of space technologies that could be employed equally by civilian and military authorities.

The centerpiece of the French efforts appears to be a large radar satellite and an operational space-based eavesdropping capacity.[42] Work has already begun on a CNES-led spaceborne radar program called Radar 2000, which eventually could be combined with a radar-equipped military satellite, called Osiris. Osiris would succeed the first-generation Helios reconnaissance spacecraft to be launched in 1994. According to the French Ministry of Defense, however, neither the radar-equipped Osiris satellite nor the Zenon eavesdropping spacecraft will be launched before the end of the decade. But the presence of the two programs in a military budget confirms that space has won a place high in the French military's priorities. An official of the DGA indicated that France hoped to turn Osiris into a European spy-satellite program, possibly organized under the auspices of the nine-nation Western European Union. Zenon would remain a purely national program.

France is already sharing the Helios satellite program with Italy and Spain. The addition of Osiris and Zenon would give France a full complement of space-based military assets at the turn of the century. French industry is also pressing for more activity in the field. Aérospatiale of Paris, the state-owned aerospace giant, has begun internal studies of an early-warning satellite that would detect the launch of missiles by an aggressor.

Federal Republic of Germany

With its civilian space program, Europe has acquired a strong position alongside the United States and what used to be the Soviet Union. The Federal Republic of Germany is not only one of the pillars of the European economic system but of European space activities as well. Playing a role in the opening up and utilization of space is extremely important for Germany for technological, scientific, economic, and political reasons.

German large-scale aerospace research is closely linked with the young history of the Federal Republic. However, its origins can be traced back to the early days of this century. The Aerodynamic Test Establishment (Aerodynamische Veruchsanstalt—AVA) was founded in Gottingen in 1907, achieving world fame in connection with the name Ludwig Prandtl. In 1969, this and other German aerospace research establishments with a long-standing tradition were combined in a single national aerospace research establishment, the DFVLR, now known as the DLR.[43] Germany also founded, in 1989, the German Space Agency (DARA) as a central management organization wholly owned by the federal government. It has the legal status of a corporation with limited liability and models its operation on the efficient management practices of private industry.

The organ responsible for advising the federal government on space policy decisions as well as on fundamental strategic and planning aspects is the Cabinet Committee on Space Activities. It advises on the allocation of the budget for space activities. Under the chairmanship of the federal chancellor, the Cabinet Committee has the following members: the head of the federal chancellery, the foreign minister, the minister of finance, the minister of economics, the defense minister, the minister of transport, the minister of research and technology, and the minister of posts and tele-communications.[44]

The Cabinet Committee's work is prepared by a State Secretaries' Committee on Space, chaired by the secretary of state in the Federal Ministry for Research and Technology (BMFT). This committee is also responsible for coordinating the space interests and activities of the various departments involved. Its members are the secretaries of state of the ministries represented on the Cabinet Committee.[45]

Representatives of the scientific community and industry are selected to form the Technical and Scientific Advisory Board. The specialized advice provided by the board ensures that scientific and economic requirements are taken into account by DARA when planning and implementing space programs.

DARA's functions can be summarized as follows:

1. To draw up plans for German space policy for approval by the federal government by:

   - planning German participation in international programs and projects;
   - planning national projects with due consideration for European, bilateral, and multilateral programs;
   - providing technological, economic, and financial recommendations, analyses, and project proposals.

2. To implement German space programs and to award industrial contracts and grants by:

   - advising the federal ministries and public institutions involved;
   - promoting, directing, and monitoring projects, and evaluating their results;
   - planning and coordination of operating facilities;
   - providing initiatives to promote commercialization;
   - allocating funds from the space budget in accordance with its statutory authority, and determining financial requirements.

3. To represent German space interests in the international arena, particularly within the European Space Agency by:

   - representing German interests on the committees of ESA and other international organizations (when this is not done at the ministerial level);
   - participating in the formulation and control of ESA's programs;
   - representing German interests in the implementation of multilateral and bilateral agreements.[46]

DARA's close partner is the above-mentioned German Aerospace Research Establishment (DLR), whose space division deals with research and development work and is also largely responsible for the operational side of space projects.

The main task of the DLR is to make a major contribution toward the scientific and technical basis for the development and utilization of future aircraft and spacecraft. To this end, not only does the DLR engage in preliminary research, but also constructs and operates large-scale test and simulation facilities, together with ground infrastructures. As a large-scale research establishment, the DLR must base its work on applications and users. Roughly two-thirds of all DLR research and development projects are handled in the form of national and international cooperation projects. Among the various forms of this international cooperation there are the exchange of information and joint symposia through the exchange of scientists and the coordination of research projects as well as the implementation of multilateral projects, the mutual utilization of test facilities, and joint development and operation of large installations. In this sense, the DLR can well be considered a member of the scientific community.

DLR's technical expertise lies with the institutes of its five scientific research departments:

1. *Flight Mechanics/Guidance and Control*

   - Institute of Flight Mechanics
   - Institute for Flight Guidance
   - Institute for Flight Systems Dynamics
   - Institute for Aerospace Medicine, Aerospace Psychology Section, Transport Research Division

2. *Fluid Mechanics*

   - Institute for Theoretical Fluid Mechanics
   - Institute for Experimental Fluid Mechanics
   - Institute for Propulsion Technology
   - Institute for Design Aerodynamics

3. *Materials and Structures*

   - Institute for Structural Mechanics
   - Institute for Aeroelasticity
   - Institute for Materials Research
   - Institute for Space Simulation
   - Institute for Structures and Design

4. *Telecommunications Technology and Remote Sensing*

   - Institute for Telecommunications
   - Institute for Radio Frequency Technology
   - Institute for Optoelectronics
   - Institute for Atmospheric Physics

5. *Energetics*

   - Institute for Technical Physics
   - Institute for Technical Thermodynamics
   - Institute for Physical Chemistry of Combustion
   - Institute for Chemical Propulsion and Chemical Engineering

As interdisciplinary installations of the DLR, the scientific-technical facilities support the institutes in their operations and system-oriented research and development tasks. The most important services include construction and operation of large-scale installations for in-house and external clients. The scientific-technical facilities include the German Space Operations Centre (GSOC) in the research center at Ober-pfaffenhofen and the divisions Crew Operations and Astronauts Office, Central Data Processing, Flight Operations and Wind Tunnels, Applied Data Technology, and the German Remote Sensing Data Center (DFD), as well as the libraries of the DLR.

The Space Vehicles, Space Applications, and Space Mission Operations sectors of the DLR play an important role in the national astronautics programs and Germany's contribution to the European projects Ariane 5, Columbus, and Hermes. DLR focuses on long-term technological activities on the construction and operation of large test facilities and the participation in the European ground infrastructure by building and operating national space centers.[47]

The Federal Republic of Germany participates in most fields of space activity. In the field of manned space flight, attention in 1993 should focus on the MIR mission—a joint project of the former Soviet Union and Germany—and the D-2 Spacelab mission, with the participation of NASA, ESA, CNES, and a consortium of Japanese firms.

In the field of space exploration, the German program is concentrated on the provision of instruments and additional flight opportunities through participation in long-term multilateral and bilateral projects. In addition, the German and European contributions to major international projects—such as the Mars mission—are also coordinated. In a field such as space exploration, continuous and comprehensive long-term studies within the framework of large-scale experiments are increasingly replacing individual projects.

In the field of launch rockets the German programs have always been realized as part of the European cooperation in ESA because the cost of developing space transport systems is beyond the means of most individual nations. The Federal Republic of Germany is also very active in the fields of satellite communications, Earth observation, space flight, and space flight systems.

Italy

In just a few years Italy has evolved into one of Europe's key space powers, dramatically increasing its spending on European Space Agency programs. At the same time, Italy's spending on domestic programs jumped significantly, as the Italian Space Agency invested billions of lire into ambitious projects.[48] Facing an enormous budget deficit and pressure from the European Community to put its finances in order, Italy has lately been forced to rein in its spending on space, but still has managed to pour huge sums into important programs.[49]

In May 1988 the Italian Parliament established the Italian Space Agency (ASI). ASI has the legal status of a public corporation, with its head office in Rome. Its activities are conducted under the supervision of the Ministry for the Coordination of Scientific and Technological Research (MRST). Its main tasks are as follows:

1. plan scientific, technological, and application programs aimed at improving the competitiveness of the national space industry;

2. provide for the formulation of the National Space Plan in accordance with the framework of European and worldwide space activities. To this end ASI is in charge of:

    • directly managing national and international programs by taking into account the capabilities as well as the level of competitiveness of public and private companies acting in the space field with public funding;

    • taking care, on the basis of MRST directives, of the national interests, both scientific and industrial, with regard to Italian participation in European Space Agency programs;

    • participating in space programs of other countries following authorization for such programs given by MRST in agreement with the Ministry of Foreign Affairs;

    • establishing relations with international or foreign space organizations to define objectives and specific cooperation activities, subject to the previous authorization of MRST as above;

    • entrusting studies, research, and actual space programs to aerospace companies, universities, and research institutes;

    • assessing and controlling projects development;

    • occasional investment in industrial concerns, public organizations, or international institutions. Such participation may be in the form of financial investment, technology, intellectual and industrial property rights, specialized personnel, or technical assistance services. Previous authorization of MRST is required;

    • promoting the circulation and utilization of information derived from space activities by providing consulting and technical assistance services to public and private entities for the utilization of space technologies, with the aim of ensuring good marketing prospects and industrial returns proportionate to the invested funds;

• promoting the training of specialized technicians in the field of space technology and relevant applications.

The Italian Space Agency has two committees appointed by the board of directors: the Scientific Committee and the Technological Committee.

The Scientific Committee has twelve members, with expertise in the space field, appointed by the National Center for Research (CNR), universities, and other scientific organizations. The committee has the task of submitting to ASI's board of directors proposals for scientific research activities. It is also in charge of providing services in the field of high-level consulting, program evaluation, and advising ASI's president on the overall activity of the agency.

The Technological Committee also has twelve members and is in charge of application programs. The selection of members is made in such a way as to ensure a balanced representation of all entities with interests in space programs and the industrial promotion of the space field.

ASI prepares the National Space Plan, which has a duration of five years but may be updated annually. The plan sets forth the activities planned by the agency as well as their estimated cost. A minimum of 15 percent of the annual plan budget is earmarked for scientific research activities.

The Interministerial Committee for Space Activities is headed by the MRST Minister and has six members, three of whom represent the Ministry of Foreign Affairs and the other three the MRST. It supports MRST in the implementation of tasks required by the participation in European and other international programs. It must be consulted in all cases where the activities of ASI are of interest to the national foreign policy. The committee is convened at least three times a year, and also upon request of the Minister for Foreign Affairs.[50]

In the hope of finding a lucrative niche in the international space market, Italy has focused on building expertise in the development of orbiting laboratories and high-technology containers that can withstand the radiation and heat of the space environment. In order to ensure that Italian companies will play an important role in the European space industry, Italy has invested heavily in the European Space Agency, so that a nearly equal amount of money will pour back into the nation's high-technology firms.

More than a decade ago Italy had its first experience in building space modules with Spacelab, built by Aeritalia together with German firms and launched on the space shuttle Columbia in 1983. Aeritalia merged with Selenia Spazio in 1991 to form Alenia Spazio. More recently, Alenia

Spazio delivered Spacelab, a pressurized module built for an American company, Spacelab, Inc. That company plans to pay for the module's travel on the space shuttle and then lease space in the module to experimenters.

A joint program between the Italian Space Agency and NASA calls for Alenia Spazio to build two logistics modules that will be used to carry equipment and experiments to the planned international space station. If the Italian government approves the program, construction will start sometime in 1993. Italy would supply the modules to NASA in exchange for flights on the shuttle, access to them for experiments, and a greater Italian role in the space station program. Alenia Spazio also has the task of building the Columbus pressurized module that will be attached to the international space station.

Italy's experience building modules could prove critical when future space contracts are assigned. In the words of ASI's President Luciano Guerriero, "a country that can afford to have space responsibilities is a country that will play a role in the world's new technology frontiers."[51]

The Netherlands

In the Netherlands, various organizations, industries, and scientific institutes are active in space research and the development of space systems.

At the government level several ministries are involved in space programs. Examples of these are the ministries of Economic Affairs, Science and Education, Transport and Public Works, and Defense. Most space activities are managed by the Netherlands Agency for Aerospace Programs (NIVR), a semigovernmental institute.

The NIVR, founded in 1946 by the Dutch government, is a semigovernmental, nonprofit agency with a statutory objective to promote industrial aerospace activities in the Netherlands. Its tasks are the following:

- To advise the government on all policy aspects of industrial aerospace activities, in particular on aircraft and space development programs;
- to initiate and monitor aerospace development programs—carried out by the Dutch aircraft and space industry—funded by NIVR and using financial resources provided by the government;
- to initiate and monitor aerospace research and technology programs—carried out by industry and by the National Aerospace Laboratory (NLR) and other research institutes—for which NIVR provides the financial resources;
- to assist the government in its function to provide appropriate representation in international organizations;

- to act as the national aerospace agency and as such deal with similar organizations in other countries.

The responsibility for the general policy of NIVR is shared by government, industry, and the scientific community who are all represented in the board of NIVR. On the government side, the following ministers appoint a board member: the minister of economic affairs, the minister of transport and public works, the minister of defense (two board members), the minister of finance, the minister of foreign affairs, and the minister of education and science. Together they appoint the chairman of NIVR. Two board members are appointed by Fokker; one board member each by Philips, Royal Dutch Airlines (KLM), and on the scientific side by the National Aerospace Laboratory (NLR) and the Netherlands Organization for Applied Research (TNO). Experts are also invited to be members of the board on a personal basis.

The Bureau of NIVR is in charge of the preparation of proposals for programs that require NIVR support, and of the supervision over such programs. It prepares and implements the decisions of the board and assures the necessary continuity in aerospace activities.

Space science activities are overviewed by the Space Research Organization Netherlands (SRON), which is a foundation within the framework of the Netherlands Organization for Scientific Research (NWO). SRON is responsible for the space research activities of the National Space Research Institute, which comprises three laboratories in Utrecht, Leiden, and Groningen. These activities range from the design, development, and building of space instruments to processing and interpretation of the data obtained with these instruments in close cooperation with university groups. In addition, SRON supports and coordinates space research in general. SRON advises the Dutch government on all activities in space research and endorses cooperation in international scientific programs, acting as the Netherlands Space Research Agency.

Most of the application projects in the field of remote sensing, meteorology, and telecommunications are controlled by the BCRS (Netherlands Remote Sensing Board), KNMI (Royal Netherlands Meteorological Institute), Rijkswaterstaat (Waterways), and the Dutch PTT.

More than fifty scientific institutes and universities are involved in space research projects. Astronomy has been a topic of main interest in the Netherlands for centuries. The Space Research Laboratories in Utrecht, Leiden, and Groningen are involved in almost all important space astronomy projects that are carried out. Scientists from various universities also play an important role in the development of instruments and the evaluation of scientific results. A dozen institutes and universities are active in the fields of meteorology, remote sensing, and geodesy. More than thirty laboratories and universities are active in the field of microgravity research.

The International Institute for Aerospace Surveys and Earth Sciences (ITC) is the largest institute for international higher education in the Netherlands. Its main objective is to assist developing countries in human resources development in aerospace surveys, remote sensing applications, the establishment of geoinformation systems, and the management of geo-information.

The Netherlands Astronautical Society was founded in 1951. It is a member of the International Astronautical Federation (IAF); one of its main objectives is to inform people about the latest developments in the field of spaceflight.[52]

Spain

Spain is a country with a healthy and growing economy, increasingly claiming its share of European success stories. A founder of the European Space Agency, Spain still conducts most of its space activities within ESA.

The Spanish institutions involved in space activities are the following:[53]

- *INTA—National Institute for Aerospace Technology.* It operates under the auspices of the Ministry of Defense. Its most important activity is R&D.
- *HISPASAT, S.A.*—It is the company that exploits the national satellite systems, and it operates under the Ministry of Public Works and Transports. It was created on June 30, 1989, as a private company.
- *TELEFONICA de ESPAÑA, S.A.*—It is the signatory party to satellite intergovernmental organizations such as INTELSAT, INMARSAT, and EUTELSAT, and it is the principal provider of satellite services in Spain.
- *CDTI—Center for the Technological and Industrial Development* of the Ministry for Industry. The center's main activity is to set industrial policy and to represent Spain in the European Space Agency.
- *DG TEL*—General Directorate for Telecommunications, a division of the Ministry of Public Works and Transports. Regulates telecommunications services and frequencies.

Switzerland

Switzerland's expenditures on space activities are mostly financed from federal funds. Parliament, the Federal Council, and the Federal Administration all tend to allocate such funds sparingly. This entails assessing carefully what is useful and necessary rather than merely desirable. Switzerland cannot keep up with the prodigious spending of the "space superpowers," but neither can it afford not to invest in areas of future promise if it wishes to obtain the benefits of technological, scientific, and also economic and social progress. It was essentially for financial reasons that Switzerland decided not to pursue a national space program. Its participation in space activities primarily takes the form of multilateral cooperation within the framework of international organizations. Switzerland thus collaborates with other European countries in major space projects far exceeding the capability of any of them. Unlike Switzerland, however, other large European countries have switched the emphasis from participation in the European Space Agency back to their national programs.

Switzerland belongs to five international space organizations. Its main efforts in the space field are devoted to the activities of the European Space Agency. In addition, Switzerland is a member of four specialized applications satellite organizations: INTELSAT, EUMETSAT, INMARSAT, and EUTELSAT. At the nongovernmental level, Swiss scientists are represented on the Standing Committee on Space Science of the European Science Foundation, ESF. This committee has an advisory role and ensures liaison among national bodies for the promotion of research, ESA, NASA, and the scientific academies of a wide variety of states. The Committee on Space Research (COSPAR) of the International Council of Space Unions (ICSU) is responsible for coordinating worldwide nongovernmental cooperation among space scientists. The Committee on Space Research of the Swiss Academy of Sciences represents the Swiss scientific community on COSPAR. Because of the traditional independence of Swiss universities and Federal Institutes of Technology, there are numerous links among researchers, institutes, the Swiss National Science Foundation, the Swiss Academy of Sciences, and their counterparts abroad. Such contacts, which do not compete with intergovernmental cooperation but rather supplement it, have enabled many Swiss scientists to take part in experiments of foreign national space agencies. [54]

Since Swiss space activities are mainly conducted under the aegis of intergovernmental organizations, it is the Federal Department of Foreign Affairs that is responsible for all the institutional, political, and legal aspects posed by such cooperation. It also handles payment of the Swiss contribution to ESA's research and development projects. On the other hand, the financial and operational aspects of participation in applications satellites organizations—e.g., INTELSAT, EUTELSAT, INMARSAT, and EUMETSAT—and in the operational activities entrusted to ESA are dealt with by the federal services directly concerned as users, namely, the General Directorate of PTT and the Swiss Meteorological Institute. The scientific aspects of Swiss cooperation in space activities fall within the responsibility of the Federal Office for Education and Science of the Federal Department of Home Affairs. It likewise insures cooperation among the relevant institutes of universities and the Federal Institutes of Technology and promotes their contacts with ESA and national space agencies.

This sharing of responsibility among the various sectors calls for close and continuous coordination of all the federal services concerned. To this end, Switzerland has created a post of permanent delegate to ESA in Paris. This continuous presence insures Swiss influence in ESA's deliberative bodies. In order to enable communities outside the administration to take part in the formulation of the aims of Switzerland's space activities, the Federal Council set up in 1963 the Federal Space Affairs Advisory Commission. In addition to federal offices and public utilities, it comprises representatives of the Swiss Council of Science Policy, the Swiss National Science Foundation, the universities and Federal Institutes of Technology, industry, the Swiss Association for Space Technology, the Swiss Academy of Sciences, and the Swiss Broadcasting Corporation.

Swiss space activities are funded from federal sources, contributions by the National Science Foundation, commitments by universities and Federal Institutes of Technology, and investments by industry. The bulk of federal outlay on space is made up of contributions to ESA's research and development programs. The agency's general budget, which includes the cost of basic technological research, and the scientific program are funded compulsorily by each member state in proportion to its net annual income, and hence to its economic potential. The National Science Foundation contributes—mainly by paying staff costs—to the scientific development of Swiss space experiments integrated into spacecraft of ESA or national space agencies and to the evaluation of the results. Such support is especially necessary for projects carried out under ESA's auspices, in which the member states' contributions to a project generally cover only the cost of the satellite and not that of its scientific equipment. The various experiments to be flown on a scientific satellite are selected on their scientific merits from among the proposals by institutes in member states, and the latter must finance them. In Switzerland, half of such funding customarily comes from the universities directly concerned, and the other half from the National Science Foundation. The latter also finances space research in physics, medicine, and biology.

Generally, space-interested firms have so far invested less in space than other industries in their respective fields. This is due partly to the great risks involved in developing products for space and partly by the limited size of this narrow and highly specialized market. Swiss industry has nevertheless devoted some of its own funds in order to compete with firms abroad. It is important for it to do so because, in other countries, applied space research is supported out of national research funds.

The United Kingdom

Britain today has an active and successful role in space, largely in partnership with the European Space Agency, to which it is the fourth largest contributor after France, Germany, and Italy. Among the main areas of space activities of interest to Britain are Earth observation, satellite communications, space transportation, and space science.

The principal space agency of Britain is the British National Space Centre (BNSC), which brings together the civil space interests of the government and research councils. It carries out the programs and projects on which the government has embarked, and advises the government on new space program proposals and opportunities as they arise. The main task of the director-general, who reports to the Secretary of State for Trade and Industry, is to provide a focus for U.K. civil space policy and to secure, by the cost effective use of resources, the maximum scientific, technological, and commercial benefit to Britain.[55] BNSC has some 235 staff operating from its London headquarters and from technical centers including RAE (the Royal Aerospace Establishment) at Farnborough, Hampshire, and RAL (the Rutherford Appleton Laboratory) at Chilton, Oxon.

Just as the U.K. is not independent in space, so BNSC is not an independent body. It is a partnership among British government departments and research councils—DTI, the above-mentioned Department of Trade and Industry; MOD, the Ministry of Defence; DoE, the Department of the Environment; the Foreign Commonwealth Office; the Cabinet Office; and the Meteorological Office; and two major Research Councils—SERC, the Science and Engineering Research Council; and NERC, the Natural Environment Research Council.

Both NERC and SERC operate under the auspices of the Department of Education and Science. The Natural Environment Research Council specializes in the scientific use of Earth observation data. A major contribution to the center is the Remote Sensing Applications Development Unit (RSADU). The objectives of RSADU are:

- to promote the use of Earth observation data through pilot demonstration programs and experimental applications;

- to transfer to a wider potential community the results of those programs;

- to provide a channel for user requirements of spaceborne systems to be fed through to instrument and platform designers;

- to provide a means of focusing the activities of the U.K. user community, for example by coordination of British Principal Investigators in the European Space Agency ERS-1 program.[56]

The current program of the unit includes the use of remote sensing in monitoring natural resources and in the study of large-scale processes, where Earth observation can provide unique information. The unit develops techniques for the extraction of physical information at the Earth's surface from the raw signal received by the satellite—for example, surface wind speed from backscattered radar power. It also undertakes a wide range of activities in support of applications of the forthcoming European Remote Sensing ERS-1 satellite and, in the longer term, the ESA Polar Orbiting Earth Observation Mission.

The Science and Engineering Research Council (SERC) provides support for universities working on a wide range of space projects that make use of facilities provided by Rutherford Appleton Laboratory (RAL). The main roles of RAL are: to support individual university groups in the design, development, testing, and operation of space instrumentation; to provide data acquisition and processing facilities; to provide project management; and to provide a working interface among universities, industries, and foreign or international space agencies such as ESA and NASA.[57]

The Earth Observation Data Centre (EODC) acts for the U.K. in handling and making available data from ERS-1 and subsequent Earth observation missions. Its development has been funded by government, and work on it (by a British Aerospace-led consortium) began in 1988. It is to be managed and operated by industry and is expected to become a self-sustaining business by 1997. EODC will be one of the four ESA Processing and Archiving Facilities established within Europe to handle data, initially from ERS-1.

In Britain, four nonnuclear Ministry of Defence research establishments were incorporated on April 1, 1991, into a new body, the Defence Research Agency (DRA).[58] DRA operates as a corporate organization, supplying on a commercial basis to the Ministry of Defence and a range of other customers an expert, comprehensive, scientific, and technical service. It has a headquarters at Pyestock, and its four main operating divisions are Portsdown, Fort Halstead, Malvern, and the Royal Aerospace Establishment at Farnborough, as well as the Royal Signals and Radar Establishment (RSRE) at Defford.

The Space Department of the Royal Aerospace Establishment is one of the BNSC Technical Centers, providing technical support and project management facilities and undertaking medium/long term space technology and remote sensing R&D programs with both civil and defense applications. Space Department work aims at developing technologies and test facilities for such programs as Olympus, ERS-1, ERS-2, and Columbus. Current space research includes overall spacecraft system design, space system reliability modeling, space data systems, novel spacecraft attitude measurement and control techniques, space robotics, reflector and phased array antennas, chemical and electrical spacecraft propulsion, studies of new forms of launch vehicles, qualification of electronic components for space use, computer modeling and measurement of the space environment, and modeling spacecraft orbital motions.

The Space Department has a comprehensive range of laboratories and test facilities including equipment designed to ensure that satellites and their subsystems will be able to perform satisfactorily in the space environment. Observation of the Earth's surface is also a major concern of the Royal Aerospace Establishment and its Space Department. Substantial civil and defense satellite remote sensing R&D programs are undertaken. A wide range of interactive analysis and data processing tools has been developed for use by visiting scientists. In addition to their spacecraft experiments, RAE staff also take part in airborne sensor trials, to evaluate applications and validate techniques and technology.

In the field of space science, which is concerned with astronomy, planetary, and solar system studies, British scientists were among the first in the world to recognize and exploit the advantages of space. Many gained international reputation and put Britain at the forefront of space research. Experienced research teams in British universities and institutes played a prominent role in several satellite missions developed over the first two decades of space exploration. Notable examples are: the U.K./U.S. Ariel 5X-ray astronomy mission; the U.S./Netherlands/U.K. Infrared Astronomy Mission, and the U.K./U.S./ESA International Ultraviolet Explorer, which was awarded the 1988 U.S. Presidential Award for Design Excellence.

Scandinavia

I. Denmark

The infrastructure for space-related activities of Denmark is not very extensive and it is basically designed to foster Danish participation in projects of the European Space Agency.

Danish membership and participation in ESA is administered by the Ministry of Education and Research. The delegation to ESA consists of officials from the International Division of the Research Department of the Ministry. The ministry also appoints a board, the Danish Space Board, which assists the ministry in laying out the strategy for participation in the various ESA programs. Another function of the board is to provide advice and guidelines for national space research. The Danish Space Research Institute was established under the auspices of the Ministry of Education and Research.[59]

II. Norway

Norway has been involved in space-related research and development for almost thirty years, reflecting a strong national interest in specific areas in this field. This involvement can draw on a range of existing industrial, technical, and scientific capabilities. Particular skills are available in such areas as computers, communications and other electronics sectors, remote sensing, cartography, construction, and materials technology as well as subsea engineering.

Official backing for Norwegian space activities both at home and abroad has been strongly enhanced by the establishment of the Norwegian Space Center in June 1987. Organized as an independent state foundation, the center was set up by the Ministry of Industry to replace the space activity division at the Norwegian Council for Scientific and Industrial Research. It works in accordance with government guidelines, for the benefit of, and in cooperation with, industry, research institutes, official agencies, and Norwegian interests in general. Its mandate includes:

- contributing to the development, coordination, and evaluation of Norwegian Space Activities;
- compiling recommendations for coordinated long-term space programs, and submitting these to the Ministry of Industry;
- managing the center's resources and efficiently distributing funds allocated by the government;
- working jointly with space-related organizations in other countries, and contributing to coordination of Norwegian and international space activities;
- representing Norway in the European Space Agency;
- coordinating space-related activities of Norwegian companies, universities and research institutes.

The Norwegian Space Center consists of three units:

1. The Oslo Headquarters;

2. The Andoya Rocket Range. This facility represents a cornerstone in Norwegian space activities. In continuous operation since 1962, the range plays a crucial role both for implementing Norway's own space research program and in projects with international cooperation. Since 1972 it has been partially funded by a number of members of the European Space Agency, who are entitled to employ the facility on a marginal cost basis.

   Other users are charged on nonprofit terms. The range has so far launched rockets and balloons primarily for investigating the upper atmosphere in the polar region. But there are plans for extending the Andoya operation into a launch facility for satellites. Launching low-cost orbital missions from Andoya offers European scientists and technologists the opportunity to prove their R&D ideas within a few hours' travel from their own laboratories;

3. The Tromso Satellite Station (TSS). At the end of 1990 TSS was reorganized and became an operational unit of the Norwegian Space Center. Considerable efforts have been put into the restructuring process. TSS is to be independently responsible for its financial budget within the Norwegian Space Center, and, in order to provide the necessary support, an internal board of directors, with members representing the headquarters and TSS, has been appointed.

The need to keep in touch with a merchant fleet spread around the world, an expanding offshore industry and remote Arctic possessions has given Norway a major stake in satellite communications. Following the lead set by the Norwegian Telecommunications Administration (NTA) in this field, a range of advanced equipment is being developed to make the best use of satcom technology.

As a major participant in INMARSAT, the NTA operates a coast earth station at Eik in southwest Norway. This facility is due to be extended to offer a range of new services, including high-speed data transmission via satellite through the Norwegian satcom system Norsat B. Eik will also serve as a base station for a new public aviation network being developed jointly with Singapore and the U.K. under the name Skyphone. The system is intended to provide air-to-ground telephone service for airline passengers.

The Norwegian Defense Research Establishment is an independent civilian research organization directly responsible to the Ministry of Defense. Its electronic division ranks as Norway's largest R&D unit in the field. The main space-related activities include: processing and analysis of earth observation, precision satellite positioning and navigation, scientific payloads for sounding rockets and satellites, telemetry systems, and electro-optical sensors.

The Center for Remote Sensing and Spatial Data-Geodatasentret A.S. is jointly owned by the Norwegian Mapping Authority, the Institute of Environmental Analysis, and private companies. It offers a wide range of services in remote sensing and geographical information systems.

ELAB is a research and development institute working on contract assignments in the fields of telecommunications, information technology, and solid state electronics. Close links are maintained with the Department of Electrical Engineering and Computer Science at the Norwegian Institute of Technology.

The Norwegian Meteorological Institute provides operational meteorological services to a range of users spanning from the oil industry to fisheries, farmers, media, government agencies, and individuals.

The Norwegian Mapping Authority handles conventional and satellite geodesy, topographic and thematic map series, charts for coastal and territorial waters, and national atlases. It reports to the Ministry of Environment.

SINTEF, the Foundation for Scientific and Industrial Research at the Norwegian Institute of Technology, provides a wide range of contract R&D services to both public and private clients. Space research developments have resulted in areas where synergy exists between space and offshore marine technology, including manned diving and submarine operations, unmanned telemanipulations, and remotely operated vehicle activities. Other space-related activities include electronics and communications work through the ELAB subsidiary listed above.

RAUFOSS A.S is a state-owned company involved mainly in pyrotechnics/solid propellants, lightweight metals, and composite materials. The company is involved in such areas as light rocket systems, missile motors, infantry, and artillery ammunition. Originally a munitions supplier, the company now also has extensive experience in development and production of defense products for the Norwegian army and NATO.[60]

III. Sweden

The Swedish National Space Board (SNSB), under the Ministry of Industry, is the central government agency responsible for national and international space activities in Sweden. For its research program the board receives funds from the Ministry of Education and Cultural Affairs. Parliament, the Telecommunications Administration, and the National Board for Technical Development, as well as industry and the scientific community, are represented on the board.

The board is responsible for:

- initiating research, development, and other activities connected with the Swedish space and remote sensing program;
- coordination of Swedish activities within the fields of space technology and research as well as remote sensing;
- distribution of government appropriations for Swedish space activities;
- maintaining contacts with international organizations and institutions operating within the field of space activities and remote sensing;
- planning and coordinating Sweden's participation in the programs of the European Space Agency.

The board has advisory committees for science, remote sensing, and industrial policy. The technical implementation of the national program is mainly delegated by the board to the state-owned Swedish Space Corporation.

The principal functions of the Swedish Space Corporation (SSC) are the following:

- the technical implementation of the Swedish space and remote sensing programs;
- to conceive and procure satellites for applications and space science research including overall project responsibility for the satellites;
- to operate the Esrange sounding rocket range and satellite ground stations;
- to perform systems management and engineering for complex high-technology programs;
- to receive image data from remote sensing satellites at Esrange. To process and analyze all types of images for different applications and customers all over the world;
- to develop and supply operational remote sensing systems for maritime surveillance and environmental control.

The Swedish Space Corporation has two facilities, one at Esrange, Kiruna, and the other in Stockholm, which is also the main office.

Space activities in Sweden are carried out at both national and international levels. The two tend to be quite interdependent. The national program consists basically of space research, remote sensing, and industrial development. The space research program comprises the publicly financed basic research activities that use sounding rockets, balloons, and satellites for their experiments. The main areas of the program are traditional space research and research in microgravity. The remote sensing program includes research and development activities pertaining to the collection, evaluation, and processing of data of the Earth and atmosphere by means of space and airborne instruments as well as ground-based equipment. The industrial development program aims at developing technical know-how in the space field in order to promote industrial competitiveness and to introduce advanced technology on the world market.

The main part of space activities at the international level is performed in cooperation with the European Space Agency. Sweden participates in the mandatory basic and science programs of ESA with a contribution rate of 3.5 percent, which is in accordance with the rules in force for the mandatory program. Sweden also participates in the optional space-application programs of ESA with contribution rates based on the expected industrial return and applications potential for each program. In particular, Sweden participates in programs pertaining to earth observation, space transportation, telecommunications, space station, and platforms and microgravity.

Sweden's financial contribution to ESA returns, to a large extent, to the country in the form of industrial development contracts and the long-term build-up of expertise. Participation in European industrial cooperation also results in access to overall achievements in the field of high technology. The returns by way of industrial contracts have been estimated to be equivalent to about two-thirds of the financial contributions that Sweden has paid to ESA and its predecessor since the 1960s. Through these contracts the Swedish space industry has been able to develop a very high competence in fields such as spaceborne data equipment, antennas, microwave technology, and rocket motors.

Sweden also engages in extensive bilateral cooperation. Bilateral cooperation with the United States is carried out under an agreement with NASA. Similarly, cooperation with the Soviet Union was carried out under a memorandum of understanding with the Intercosmos Council of the Soviet Academy of Sciences. Cooperation with France takes place under an agreement with the Centre National d'Études Spatiales (CNES). Memoranda of Understanding have been signed as a basis for cooperation with Austria, Canada, India, and the People's Republic of China. Sweden is also engaged in other bilateral co-operative projects with Denmark, Finland, Italy, Japan, the Netherlands, Norway, Switzerland, and the United Kingdom.

The Swedish Institute of Space Physics (IRF) has been working in Kiruna since 1957 and now has departments in Uppsala, Umea, and Lycksele. The institute employs about sixty-five persons in Kiruna and is the largest recipient of funds from SNSB's national space research program.

Esrange, the space research range situated north of the Arctic Circle, was established in the 1960s by ESA's predecessor as a launching site for sounding rockets. Since 1972 the Swedish Space Corporation has been responsible for the operation of the base. Activities are carried out as an ESA special project with the Federal Republic of Germany, France, Switzerland, Norway, and Sweden as participating states.

Due to the geographical location, studies of the aurora and other high-latitude phenomena are of particular interest. Land recovery possibility makes Esrange very suitable for all sounding-rocket experiments needing recovery, such as those in microgravity research. Esrange is also used in various types of satellite experiments. A number of ground segments for the support of national and international spacecraft programs are now in operation or under development.

A facility for the reception, recording, filing, processing, and dissemination of remote sensing satellite data was established at Esrange in 1978. This station was originally used for spacecraft in the Landsat series and operated within the framework of ESA's Earthnet program. The station has been extended to handle data from both remote sensing and scientific satellites and has several independent antennas and processing systems. A satellite control station of universal design performs operations on orbiting satellites. Esrange operates and monitors satellites on behalf of customers or offers use of the station in a transparent mode where remote customers are connected to the station for real-time access to their satellites.[61]

Eastern Europe

The political transformation of the countries of Eastern Europe also changed their respective roles and alliances in the field of space activities.[62] Since 1967 these countries have relied on Soviet rockets, satellites, and tracking systems that were later made available in the context of the Intercosmos cooperation (pursuant to the Agreement on Cooperation in the Exploration and Use of Outer Space for Peaceful Purposes, signed in Moscow on July 13, 1976).

The function of Intercosmos, which lacked the common funding and other characteristics of an international organization proper, was to coordinate national space research bodies set up by each member government. A meeting of chairmen of national space organizations, which represented their countries, oversaw the various projects. The original program of Intercosmos was oriented to basic research conducted in scientific institutes but later evolved into a more user-oriented applied research mechanism. The program began by including space physics, meteorology, biology and medicine, communications, and the environment. It gradually expanded and became a multidisciplinary network among institutes, universities, ministry research institutions, and laboratories. Intercosmos is still in existence today and it enables cooperation with any partners, within or without the original membership of the organization.

In the case of Czechoslovakia, as of 1991 it had participated, mainly through Intercosmos, in over 140 experiments in space physics, space biology and medicine, and remote sensing. The construction of most of the space instruments involved in those experiments was done in cooperation with partners from both Eastern and Western Europe. While the future of Intercosmos is uncertain in view of the political developments, individual projects already under way continue, despite funding and other difficulties. At the same time, existing scientific and technical teams are forming closer ties to other space programs, particularly in Europe. In 1990, for example, Czechoslovakia signed an agreement with the French CNES on Earth observation and other space research cooperation. Also, on February 11, 1992, EUMETSAT and the Czech and Slovak Hydrometeorological Services concluded a four-year agreement on the use of Meteosat images and data free of charge.

All the former socialist countries of Europe are moving toward closer cooperation with the European Space Agency. Hungary concluded a Cooperation Agreement with ESA in 1990, and similar agreements have been negotiated with Poland and Romania though they have not yet been signed; Czechoslovakia was engaged in similar negotiations in June of 1992. The aim of those proposed agreements is cooperation in space science, research and applications of remote sensing, telecommunications, microgravity research, and material processing. Other provisions deal with working-level consultations on joint projects, awards and fellowships, exchanges of experts, and joint symposia.

The domestic developments in the countries of Eastern Europe have pointed to the necessity of establishing institutions comparable to the space agencies of other countries. Hungary decided early in 1992 to establish a space research agency and Poland is also considering such a step. Czechoslovakia has established a commission, chaired by the president of the Czechoslovak Academy of Sciences, but it now believes the commission should be replaced by an agency with the functions of a coordinating and advisory body of the government that would act as the government's representative in international relations.

In 1968 the Romanian Commission for Space Activities (CRAS) was created as a representative organization at the government level and active in Intercosmos.[63] After the 1989 revolution, favorable conditions developed for the growth of international cooperation that led to the creation, in February 1992, of the Romanian Space Agency (ASR) under the Ministry of Science and Education. The agency is in charge of coordinating national space programs and representing the government in the relations with similar organizations of other countries. ASR is active within the United Nations bodies that deal with outer space matters and is negotiating a cooperation agreement with ESA.

THE FORMER SOVIET UNION

The upheaval and turmoil that saw the world change in the last few years has not left the space field untouched. Particularly in the case of the Soviet Union, radical changes have taken place that mirror the transition between a single, major superpower to a loose alliance of independent states. What was the unquestioned cooperation and synergy between closely knit republics is now replaced by more or less temporary agreements that follow the vagaries of international politics. Even as this book goes to press, the evolution of the former Soviet Union continues and will probably continue for some time to come. What is described below is therefore only an attempt to describe the main trends of the current post-Soviet situation.

Whatever new alliances and agreements may be formed in the future, including cooperation with the West and a reduction in space activities, it is this writer's opinion that the bulk of what used to be an incredible space program will be more than a legacy. It will somehow survive the turmoil and find new patrons in the new political order.

Taking into account the economic, scientific, and technical legacy of the Soviet space program, there are important incentives to carry out space activities jointly among member states of the Commonwealth of Independent States (CIS) on the basis of treaties of an international character among those members that are interested. A first such treaty—the Agreement on Combined (Joint) Activities in the Exploration and Use of Outer Space—was concluded in Minsk at the highest level among CIS member states on December 30, 1991, almost simultaneously with the CIS's creation.[64] As of August 1992, all member states of the CIS except Moldova have signed the agreement.

The Minsk Agreement is, in part, a general statement. It notes the necessity of developing space activities, the significance of space science and technology for the development of the Commonwealth, and the need for combined efforts. The interests to be served are the economy, science, defense, and the collective security of CIS member states. But the accord also indicates how the combined efforts should be undertaken. Joint activities are to be effected on the basis of interstate programs of space research and exploration, the implementation of which is to be coordinated by a special organ—the Interstate Space Council. Interstate programs for military or dual use purposes will rely on the Joint Strategic Armed Forces for their fulfillment. The agreement also provides principles for the continuing utilization of space facilities, proportionate financing, and associated functional questions.

On May 15, 1992, a new agreement was signed in Tashkent by all CIS member states except Moldova. This treaty develops some provisions of the Minsk Agreement, particularly over ground infrastructure for space programs. One of its main provisions, Article 1, which was the subject of considerable differences, stipulates that ground facilities (such as the Baikonur and Plesetsk cosmodromes, the Cosmonauts Training Center, technical, launch and landing complexes, and flight control centers) that are situated on the territories of Azerbaijan, Belarus, Kazakhstan, Russia, Turkmenistan, Uzbekistan, and the Ukraine are to be considered property of those states. The right to use these facilities is transferred to strategic forces of CIS or other parties concerned on the basis of special agreements.

On May 25, 1992, Russia and Kazakhstan signed a bilateral agreement on the problems connected with the utilization of Baikonur Cosmodrome, which is situated in Kazakhstan and is property of that state. The agreement not only governs access and use conditions to Baikonur, but also provides a basis for coordination of space programs. Other matters are also dealt with, such as financial procedures and ecological and social issues.

The combination of the Minsk, Tashkent, and Baikonur agreements has regulated some of the most pressing problems connected with the transition from the old to the new order but the challenge remains one of establishing a full-scale cooperative program within the CIS, assuming, of course, that the CIS will indeed be a permanent feature of the new political structure.

In the overall post-Soviet situation, it is Russia that is taking over the bulk of the Soviet space program. In February 1992, President Boris Yeltsin issued a decree on the creation of the Russian Space Agency. In April, the Russian government established the powers of this organ, which has been charged with the elaboration and realization of Russian space policy. More specifically, the functions of the Russian Space Agency are:

- the elaboration, in collaboration with other bodies, of a draft space program;
- the promotion of commercial space activities;
- the development of cooperation with CIS member states and other countries in the exploration and use of outer space.

In addition to this first organizational step, President Yeltsin also approved a number of other measures aimed at developing Russian space activities, both in administrative and legislative terms. The most significant move was the decision to go ahead with the drafting of a Space Act for the Russian Federation. The task of producing a draft was given to the Russian Academy of Sciences (Institute of State and Law) assisted by other bodies. The draft, which is to be submitted to parliament, has the goal of determining:

- the guiding principles for the conducting of space activities;
- the competence of the president, government, parliament, Russian Space Agency, and other Russian institutions active in this field;
- the status of the space program and the means for financing space activities.

The Space Act would also regulate some other questions deriving from obligations under international law, such as the legal status of space objects and astronauts, and the allocation of liability and responsibility for the exploration and use of outer space. More specific norms, however, will be required to deal with the numerous details involved and it is likely that they will be enacted following the adoption of the Space Act.

Among Russia's major space enterprises are:

- the Central Specialized Design Bureau (CSDB) of Samara, Russia, which leads development of military satellites and Earth observation;
- NPO Energia of Kaliningrad, outside Moscow, which is responsible for heavy-lift launchers and Russia's cosmonaut program;
- NPO Applied Mechanics of Krasnoyarsk, in Siberia, which manages the development of communications satellites;
- KB Yushnoye of Dniepropetrovsk, in Ukraine, which handles military launch vehicles and the Zenit rocket program;
- KB Machine Building, of Moscow, responsible for the Proton launch vehicle; and
- a design bureau located at Miass, in the Urals, which manages ocean-observation technologies.

The Soviet space program was a major accomplishment for that country. Although there is now some institutional and political confusion and a serious cash shortage, the major activities continue in one form or another.

Before its dissolution, the Union of Soviet Socialist Republics publicly admitted to launching eight space stations, each nonmilitary. Upon closer examination, however, the actual number of launches was much larger than that, with some being military in nature.[65] In the late 1960s and early 1970s, the Soviets focused on four major manned space programs—circumlunar missions; lunar landing missions, and two separate space station programs, one a highly visible program, the other a classified one. During this period, the USSR aggressively developed military space systems such as a fractional orbit bombardment system and a satellite interceptor system. In addition, a new generation of strategic rocket forces missiles were under development. Starting in 1969, resources shifted away from the manned circumlunar program to manned station programs.

On April 19, 1971, Salyut 1 was launched. On April 3, 1973, Salyut 2 was orbited. Unlike Salyut 1, which transmitted on radio frequencies used by previous manned spacecraft, this station transmitted on frequencies used by Soviet photoreconnaissance spacecraft. On June 22, 1976, Salyut 5 was orbited. It hosted two manned missions: Soyuz 21 for forty-nine days and Soyuz 24 for eighteen days. A third mission, Soyuz 23, failed to dock at the station. On February 26, 1977, the day after the last crew departed, a recoverable capsule was separated from the station and on August 8, Salyut 5 was commanded to reenter. There has been little information released on these three stations and their missions but they appear to have been tests of classified, people-tended, automated, photoreconnaissance station missions, similar to the proposed United States Air Force Manned Orbiting Laboratory of the 1960s.

Many other missions were conducted in the years that followed including the Salyut B, Cosmos, and the Almaz 1A, launched in 1991. As late as mid-1991 there were still ambitious projects for the space program. Supporters of these programs have pointed out that technological spinoffs have helped the Soviet economy along with strides made in basic research. The Minsk Agreement and the other agreements that followed show that there is support for these programs from the political leadership of most of the CIS in spite of the serious domestic problems each of the republics is now facing.

One of the early challenges facing the CIS is the aging Mir space station complex, which will require substantial maintenance in the future. It will be difficult if not impossible for the CIS to continue the Mir program without substantial funding from the West. The European Space Agency may come to the rescue by using the Russian space station the way it uses Spacelab aboard the U.S. space shuttle. The agency also announced an increased emphasis on cooperation with Russia on other activities, including a joint Euro-Russian piloted space shuttle to be developed in the late 1990s. A decision on this will not be made until 1995, however, following three years of space plane studies by the European Space Agency and several Russian organizations. The agency has proposed spending about $150 million for the next three years on contracts with Russian companies to explore possible areas of cooperation.

ESA has also opened negotiations with NPO Energia of Kaliningrad on widening ESA's role in Russia's space station program. ESA plans to send astronauts to Russia's Mir space station in the mid-1990s and to build limited hardware for the planned Mir 2 station, foreseen in the latter half of this decade. By 2005 at the earliest, the agency would like to join Russia as a full partner in the construction of a new space station, which could be visited by the Euro-Russian shuttle.[66]

From the institutional point of view, the space programs of Europe and Russia have taken a decisive step toward a form of merger with Russia's request for associate membership in the European Space Agency. Events are moving so quickly that no one can say where the process of cooperation might end. The pace of change is dictated by different needs on each side. ESA must come up with a trimmed-down, less expensive, long-term program. Preliminary investigations suggest that former Soviet space hardware can be purchased for half of what it would cost in Western Europe. In Russia, the once-privileged space infrastructure risks withering in the reality of a market economy where profit and loss matter a great deal.[67]

The United States has also expressed interest in cooperation with its former adversary. NASA planners are focusing on a September 1994 shuttle flight to rendezvous with the Russian Mir space station and possibly bring back a U.S. astronaut launched to the outpost earlier that summer aboard a Soyuz rocket.[68] Launch is tentatively scheduled for September 9, 1994, after extensive modifications to install a Russian docking fixture in the shuttle Atlantis's cargo bay.

Other areas of space activities are in serious jeopardy unless the West can help fund them. Russia's plans to explore Mars this decade with two research spacecraft could be postponed or canceled unless about $10 million in financial aid from NASA and other Western space agencies is found. The Mars '94 and Mars '96 missions would send robotic spacecraft and scientific instruments to study the surface and the atmosphere of Mars. The missions are to be launched by Proton expendable rockets. Current plans call for the Mars '94 spacecraft to consist of an orbiter filled with various scanners, cameras, and electronic gear along with a descent module to land two small, stationary scientific stations and two subsurface probes. The more ambitious Mars '96 mission includes a similar orbiting satellite and a larger descent-module payload. It includes the robotic rover vehicle, a Mars balloon, and two or four more scientific stations and ground penetrators.[69]

As indicated earlier, one of the ways the Russian space industry fights for its survival is to offer prices for its space hardware and services that are below those of Western Europe and the United States. In a recent contract bid for a Western commercial satellite launch, Russian authorities have offered a price that is more than 40 percent lower that those of the American and European competition. KB Salyut of Moscow, which designs Russia's Proton launch vehicle, has offered to orbit an Inmarsat-3 satellite in the mid-1990s for $35 million. This compares to bids of between $60 million and $65 million offered by General Dynamics Commercial Launch Services of San Diego, and Europe's Arianespace consortium of Evry, France. Breaking with a long-standing prohibition, the U.S. government agreed in June 1992 to permit Russia to launch one commercial U.S.-built satellite. The sixty-four-nation International Maritime Satellite Organization of London, of which Russia is a member, has for several years pressed for the right to consider Russian rockets and now is free to do so.[70]

Although Russia is clearly the republic that inherited the bulk of the Soviet space program, other newly independent republics are gradually taking responsibility in their own right for a share of space activities. The Ukraine is looking both east and west to rescue its threatened space industry. Ukrainian space officials said they intend to cooperate closely with their traditional Russian partners, but the government is also considering ties to the European Space Agency and seeking commercial contracts with the United States.[71]

The Ukraine has several major space facilities, including a factory that produces the Zenit rocket, but the economic circumstances are so bad that it is difficult for the new country to organize its own space agenda. The National Space Agency of the Ukraine was set up in May of 1992 and its budget and direction has not yet been decided by parliament.

Sandwiched between Russia on the east and Czechoslovakia and Romania on the west, the Ukraine is seeking stronger ties with the West while building a new relationship with Russia. In order to find international support, the country is trying to develop closer cooperation with France, Sweden, and ESA and is considering applying for membership in ESA.

Because of the financial problems confronting the government, the new space program is expected to pay for itself through contracts with foreign countries and companies. The Ukraine can offer inexpensive satellite components and scientific instruments, as well as the Zenit launcher. The country also has extensive expertise in solar research and remote-sensing platforms that could prove beneficial to Western space science.

In spite of its overtures to Europe and the United States, the Ukraine will remain linked to the Russian space program and the Baikonur launch site in Kazakhstan. NPO Yuzhnoye, where thousands of workers built some of the Soviet Union's most advanced ballistic missiles, is a major subcontractor of NPO Energia based outside Moscow, and other Ukrainian companies are subcontractors of Russian organizations.[72]

As noted earlier, Kazakhstan's major claim to the space program of the former Soviet Union is the Baikonur cosmodrome, which has been a source of major controversy between that republic and Russia. Yielding to Kazakh pressure, Russian space officials have agreed to pay Kazakhstan a portion of the profits from future visits to Russia's Mir space station. Other concessions have also been made to ensure that the largest launch site of the former Soviet Union is maintained. Russian authorities have operated Baikonur since the 1950s with minimal Kazakh participation. Missions to the Mir space station are launched from here aboard Soyuz rockets, and separate launch sites have been built for the Energia vehicle and its Buran shuttle, and for Zenit and Proton rockets. The main complaint of Kazakhistan is that it does not have enough say in the management of the facility and does not share in the launch profits.[73]

Following the bilateral agreement between Russia and Kazakhistan of May 25, 1992, mentioned earlier, Russia will pay Kazakh authorities 15 percent of the profits from the sale of Mir visits to international customers. Russia will be responsible for paying 94 percent of the yearly operation of the facility, which, before the break-up of the Soviet Union, was estimated at $20 million. Kazakhstan will pay the remaining 6 percent. In addition, Russia's NPO Energia design bureau, which manages Mir operations and employs about 2,000 permanent staff at Baikonur, will start a preferential hiring program to train locals in the management of the launch facility.[74]

PEOPLE'S REPUBLIC OF CHINA

The activities of China in the space field date back to the 1950s when the government formulated a development plan for the space industry and the related scientific research organizations. In 1964 China launched its first launch vehicle, marking the country's entry into the space age.[75] On April 24, 1970, China sent its first satellite into Earth orbit using the LM-1 launch vehicle. This was followed by the successful launching of the Shi Jian 1 satellite on March 3, 1971. On November 26, 1975, China for the first time launched a recoverable satellite using an LM-2C launch vehicle.

In April 1984 and February 1986 an experimental communications satellite and a broadcasting satellite were launched with LM-3 launch vehicles. China has thus far successfully launched thirty satellites with self-developed launch vehicles. These satellites serve a variety of purposes and were sent into different orbits. A professional team with full research and development, production, and testing capabilities has emerged in the process. China now possesses the Long March family of launch vehicles, three launch centers, and a satellite network including tracking ships. All this has led to an independent and comprehensive space industrial system.

Among the government institutions dealing with space activities are the following:

- Chinese Academy of Sciences;
- Chinese Academy of Space Technology;
- State Science and Technology Commission, National Remote Sensing Center;
- Commission of Science Technology and Industry for National Defense;
- Ministry of Aerospace Industry;
- Ministry of Post and Telecommunications.

Under the auspices of those institutions, there are a number of other entities that actually carry out space activities.

Organizations Responsible for Launch Services

China Great Wall Industry Corporation (CGWIC), a foreign trade company under the Ministry of Aerospace Industry of China, registered under the laws of China, is the sole organization in China responsible for launch-service marketing, commercial negotiation, contract execution, and performance. It deals in the import and export of Chinese astronautics technology and products. It has a wide scope of business, the major aspects of which are launch services and satellite applications. CGWIC's partners and subcontractors include:

- China Satellite Launch and TT&C General (CLTC)
- Beijing Wan Yuan Industry Corporation (BWYIC)
- Shanghai Bureau of Astronautics (SHBOA)
- Chinese Academy of Space Technology (CAST)

China Satellite Launch and TT&C General is an organization under the Commission of Science, Technology and Industry for National Defense, responsible for satellite launches and TT&C services. CLTC runs three satellite launch centers located in Jiuquan, Xichang, and Taiyuan; one satellite control center located in Xian; and a global TT&C network. In addition, it operates two research institutes: Luoyang Institute of Tracking and Telecommunications Technology and Beijing Special Engineering & Design Institute. The total workforce of CLTC is over 20,000, of which some 5,000 are engineers.

Beijing Wan Yuan Industry Corporation, under the Ministry of Aerospace Industry of China, is responsible for the development, production and testing of launch vehicles. BWYIC is a large institution with thirteen research institutes and six factories. It has full capability for the independent development, design, and testing of launch systems. It can handle the complete production process from parts manufacturing to integrated assembly. In support of CGWIC, the prime contractor of launch services, BWYIC is responsible for technical coordination, providing technical documents for the execution of launch services. It also provides on-site technical supervision for the testing of the launch vehicle and actual launching.

The Chinese Academy of Space Technology engages in the development of satellites. The academy has succeeded in developing a number of scientific research satellites and application satellites. It has acquired advanced technology for satellite recovery, multisatellites launching with one launch vehicle, and fixed positioning of geosynchronous communications satellites. The research institutes and factories under CAST have full capability in undertaking the development, design, and production of various types of application satellites, sounding rockets, and related technical engineering projects. These units can also supply technology and equipment to users in the fields of vacuum, low temperature, automatic control, remote sensing, radio, and precision machinery.

The Shanghai Bureau of Astronautics is a research and production base of the Ministry of Aerospace Industry in the Shanghai area. It supervises ten research institutes and twelve factories, comprising a total work force of over 30,000, of which some 6,000 are engineering and technical personnel. The bureau undertakes the development and production of the attitude control system of the LM-3 launch vehicle, and the inertia components and instruments for the guidance and stabilization system. The LM-4, a large launch vehicle with constant-temperature liquid propellant developed by the bureau, has already been used for the successful launch of China's SSO meteorological satellite in September 1988.

Remote Sensing Applications. The government of China pays great attention to the development of space technology applications, especially in the field of remote sensing, which is a very useful tool for natural resources and environmental management in a country with such a large population.

As of the early 1950s, China started using aerial remote sensing for surveying and mapping, geological exploration, railroad route selection, and other purposes.[76] In the 1970s China started extensive research on the applications of space and aerial remote sensing, which included field spectral measurements, research on remote sensors, image processing equipment, and applied experiments. By the end of the seventies, satellite data began to be used for natural resources and environmental evaluation. At the same time, some comprehensive application experiments of satellite remote sensing provided useful information for many government departments. During the past decade, the emphasis of Chinese remote sensing development was on fundamental research, development of new sensors, image processing techniques, and remote sensing applications. A number of experimental application projects have been successfully undertaken in agriculture, forestry, hydrology, geology, oceanology, and urban planning with significant social and economic benefits. From 1981 to the present, some remote sensing organizations have been established in the country. Also, a preliminary remote sensing data acquisition system, data processing system, and data application network have been set up. Remote sensing information has been widely used in many important areas in the country.

At present, China has more than 180 remote sensing organizations across the academic, research, educational, industrial, and other sectors. The National Remote Sensing Centre (NRSC) was established in April, 1981 and is in charge of:

- organizing studies on policies of remote sensing development and formulating related technical policies;
- drawing up national, long-term, remote sensing plans;
- coordinating remote sensing activities and projects;
- identifying priority development projects;
- promoting technical training and consultation services; and
- promoting and coordinating international projects.

The NRSC consists of eight departments with more that 3,000 scientists and engineers, in the fields of research and development, technical training, information service, satellite remote sensing ground stations, aerial remote sensing, and geographical information systems. Many specialized remote sensing application agencies have also been set up by regional governmental departments and ministries such as the Water Resources

Remote Sensing Center, the Geological Remote Sensing Center, and some provincial remote sensing centers. Their main goal is to apply remote sensing technology to social and economic development.

Among the main areas of remote sensing applications are the following:

1. Natural Disaster Monitoring and Evaluation, which includes:

    * flood monitoring;
    * forest fires;
    * earthquakes;
    * drought;
    * integrated inventory of the "Three-North" Forest Shelter Belt;
    * integrated inventory of soil erosion in the Loess Plateau.

2. Development for Remote Sensing Image Processing;
3. National Digital Terrain Model (DTM) Data Base;
4. Space Remote Sensing Data Acquisition System;
5. Evaluation of Mineral Resources;
6. Applications of Remote Sensing in Surveying and Mapping;
7. Technical Training.

The eighth five-year plan (1991–1995) of the National Science and Technology Development Program includes the following areas:

* Applications Relating to Damage Control for Natural Disasters;
* Monitoring of Global Environment Changes;
* Yield Estimation for Main Crops;
* New Sensors Research and Development;
* Technical Training; and
* International Cooperation.

Satellite Communications. The strategy for communications satellites development and application is set by the central government of China. The State Science and Technology Commission is responsible for organizing and coordinating research and technology development. The Ministry of Post and Telecommunications handles the implementation of the plans for communication satellites. Private communications networks are established by users according to their own requirements. Industrial concerns are responsible for the manufacturing of satellites and Earth station equipment.

Satellites have become a very important means of international communications for China. From 1973 to 1992, China established six INTELSAT A-type Earth stations (four in Beijing and two in Shanghai), which use the INTELSAT satellites located above the Pacific and Indian Oceans for international telecommunications to link China with more than 150 countries and regions. For domestic communications, China has established several Earth stations in Beijing, Nanjing, Shanghai, and Hohhot. On April 12, 1984, China launched its first experimental communications satellite, which started an experimental satellite communications network.

The use of satellites for TV systems contributed to communications satellites development in China. From fifty-three TVRO stations in 1985, the number has risen to 30,000. That growth is also due to educational uses of television aimed at classrooms and at teachers of primary to high schools. More than 3 million people have received on-the-job training and continuing education and more than 20 million farmers have learned practical farming technology from satellite TV education programs.

By August 1992 China had established a satellite communication system to serve the public network, which consists of seven large Earth stations in large urban areas and more than 100 large ones in remote areas. The private network is growing even faster than the public one. The existing networks include: a petroleum telephone network, a power telephone network, coal telephone network, a central bank data network, and a news and newspaper data network.

China plans to give a boost to business communications via satellite in the future. The number of transponders will soon reach fifty and there will be nineteen large Earth stations for regional centers. By that time, the major cities in China will be linked by about 8,000 satellite communication circuits with digital technology. The government also intends to establish an emergency satellite communication system.

JAPAN

Today, Japan stands with a select handful of countries around the world at the forefront of progress in space. Its advanced technology, state-of-the-art ground control network, and fleet of satellites represent a distinguished record of achievements.

Japan's space program got off the ground with the launching of its first rocket in 1970. The National Space Development Agency of Japan (NASDA) followed that success with new programs of space research and experiments, the beginning of two decades of building a firm foundation for the future. The 1970s saw Japan heavily in the debt of American know-how, as NASDA borrowed propulsion and other systems technology from the United States. Working in cooperation with American industry, the result was an impressive series of successes in satellite and launch vehicle development. These efforts paid dividends in the 1980s as Japan began relying primarily on its own technology in liftoff, tracking, and downrange operations.

As Japan consolidates its position as one of today's leading information societies, the demand for satellite services is skyrocketing. More and more television viewers, for instance, are tuning in to programs offering new audio and visual quality, thanks to satellite broadcasting. And communications satellites are fast becoming the backbone of a burgeoning new industry of communication services that are changing the face of contemporary business.[77]

Japan's space development is conducted in accordance with the long-term guidelines stated in the Fundamental Policy of Japan's Space Development established by the Space Activities Commission. The Space Development Program is formulated according to the policy and provides specific space programs. The Fundamental Policy was established in March 1978 and updated in June 1989. The Fundamental Policy, as updated, defines directions and goals for the next ten years. The fundamental principles can be summarized as follows.

* Response to changing and diversifying needs.
* Establishment of the technological foundation required to conduct space development activities consistent with Japan's role in the international community.
* Encouragement of the private sector to obtain sufficient capability.

The specific objectives are the following:

* Promotion of scientific research.
* Establishment of satellite and rocket technology.
* Creation of a basis for utilization of the space environment and the international space station.
* Creation of foundation for manned space activities.

The institutional framework for space activities includes the following organizations.

Space Activities Commission. The Space Activities Commission (SAC) was established within the Prime Minister's Office in 1968 under the Law for the Establishment of SAC, to develop the activities of the National Space Activities Council, which had been operational since 1960. Its purpose was to unify space activities of various government agencies and actively promote them.

SAC plans, deliberates, and makes decisions on matters detailed below and submits its opinions to the prime minister for final decisions. The prime minister takes into account the opinions submitted by SAC. The field of competence of SAC includes the following:

- important policy matters regarding space activities;
- important matters related to the overall coordination of space-related work among government agencies concerned;
- estimates of space activity expenses of the government agencies concerned.
- matters related to cultivation and training of space researchers and engineers.

SAC consists of five men of learning including the minister of state for science and technology, who serves as its chairman (its members are nominated by the prime minister based on the approval of the Legislative Assembly). Its secretariat functions are performed by the Research and Development Bureau of the Science and Technology Agency.

Science and Technology Agency. The agency, also known as STA, established the Space Science and Technology Preparation Office in May 1960, thereby including space activities for the first time in a governmental organization of Japan. In July 1964, it set up the National Space Development Center and commenced full-fledged activities as the main promoter of Japan's space activities.

In order to achieve more efficiency in space activities, the agency reorganized the National Space Development Center into the National Space Development Agency of Japan (NASDA), which hired able personnel from industrial, academic, and governmental circles.

STA now plans, regulates, and promotes the basic space-related policy, overall coordination of space activities among government agencies, and conducts research and development activities through the National Aerospace Laboratory (NAL), a research organization attached to it, and NASDA. It thereby plays the central role in Japan's space activities.

National Aerospace Laboratory (NAL). NAL, originally called the National Aeronautical Laboratory, was established in July 1955 as a subsidiary organization of the Prime Minister's Office to expedite the redevelopment of aeronautical technology. After STA was established in 1956, NAL was placed under its administration. In 1963 NAL was charged with the additional task of conducting research in space technology and given its present name—National Aerospace Laboratory.

NAL established its Rocket Division in 1963, and its Kakuda Research Center in 1966 to allow research on a wider scope. The Rocket Division was reorganized into the Space Technology Research Group in October 1969 to permit more effective advancement of space technology with a stronger organization. Since then, the Space Technology Research Group and the Kakuda Research Center have been the central bodies of technology advancement in NAL, although close cooperation with other divisions is occasionally required. Most NAL divisions are involved in the research of the key technologies for the space plane, which NAL considers essential to Japanese autonomous space activities in the twenty-first century.

NAL has strong connections with NASDA, with which it jointly conducts various experiments essential to space development. NAL offers its research data to other organizations to promote further space development. It also undertakes basic as well as advanced studies that are considered crucial to future progress in space activities.

The principal activities of NAL in space technology are as follows:

- Research on basic technologies of spaceplanes in the fields of aerodynamics, advanced composite structures, flight control, propulsion systems, manned space activities, and orbiter maneuvering engines;
- Joint research with NASDA on aerodynamics, guidance and control, and structure for the design of the H-II Orbiting Plane (HOPE).
- Research on oxygen-hydrogen rocket engine components.
- Research on satellite systems and space environment utilization.

National Space Development Agency of Japan (NASDA). NASDA was established in October 1969 under the NASDA law as the central space development implementation organization of Japan, to promote space activities for peaceful purposes.

NASDA's main tasks are to develop artificial satellites and their launching vehicles; to launch and track satellites; and to devise methods, facilities, and organizations for these purposes in accordance with the Space Development Program. To perform those tasks, NASDA has facilities in various parts of the country including the following.

- Tenegashima Space Center. Tenegashima has a total land area of 8.6 million square meters. The site has a launch pad for large, liquid-propelled rockets such as the H-I. It also has various facilities for communication as well as optical, radio wave, and test systems. There are also ground combustion test facilities for checking the reliability of liquid-propelled rocket engines and their parts as well as their performance within the launch site. To track and support the rockets launched, two radar stations are located on Tenegashima Island.

- Yoshinobu (H-II) Launch Complex. Major facilities and equipment include a vehicle assembly building, mobile launcher, pad service tower, propellant storage and supply facilities, and a launch control building.

- Tsukuba Space Center. The construction of the center began in 1970 in Tsukuba Science City and many new facilities have been added in the area of 510,000 square meters. Furnished with up-to-date equipment, the center conducts research and development in space technology and engineering tests of satellites and launch vehicles. It also plays an important role as the tracking and control center for Japanese satellites. A large-capacity computing system facilitates various types of analyses and real-time data processing during launch and initial orbit phases. Other roles of the center include collecting and maintaining information and data concerning space development, as well as providing education and training and implementing joint studies with other organizations.

- Kakuda Propulsion Center. This facility is responsible for research and development of rocket parts. Its main task at present is to develop LE-7, the first stage engine for the H-II rocket.

- Earth Observation Center. This facility receives and processes remote sensing data utilizing artificial satellites. It now receives and processes data from Japan's Marine Observation Satellite-1, U.S. LANDSAT, and French SPOT.

Institute of Space and Astronautical Science (ISAS), Ministry of Education. ISAS is a central institute for space and astronautical science in Japan. It conducts scientific research using space vehicles. For this purpose, it develops and operates sounding rockets, satellite launchers, scientific satellites, planetary probes, and scientific balloons. As of 1990, eighteen scientific and test satellites have been launched including "Suisei" and "Sakigake," which explored Halley's comet in 1986.

ISAS was founded in April 1981 by the reorganization of the Institute of Space and Aeronautical Science, University of Tokyo, which was the core of Japanese space research from 1964 to 1981. The present ISAS is a national research institute that operates directly under the auspices of the Ministry of Education, Science, and Culture. ISAS takes part in graduate education and has its main campus at Sagamihara. Other ISAS centers scattered around the country are the following:

- Kagoshima Space Center (KSC). This site is located in Uchinoura-cho, which lies on the east coast of Ohsumi Peninsula, Kagoshima Prefecture. It includes various facilities, such as those for launching rockets, telemetry, tracking, and command stations for rockets and satellites and optical observation posts. As of 1990 the center had launched a total of 330 rockets.

- Noshiro Testing Center. This site was established in 1962 on Asanai Beach, Noshiro City, Akita Prefecture. The ground firing test stand, workshop, measurement center, optical observatory, and other facilities are provided for ground-based firing tests of large-scale solid motors.

- Usuda Deep Space Center. This center is located in Usuda-machi, Nagano Prefecture. It is at an elevation of 1,450 meters and is surrounded by mountains that block out city noises. This site started operating in October 1984. A sixty-four meter parabolic antenna receiver, transmitter, and ranging system in S-band serve as a deep-space tracking, telemetry, and command station. These facilities can be controlled by the Deep Space Operation Center of ISAS's main campus in Sagamihara, Kanagawa.

- Sanriku Balloon Center. This site is located in Sanriku-cho, which is on the east coast of Iwate Prefecture facing the Pacific Ocean. The balloon launch site is situated on a hill 230 meters above sea level. The control center is located beside the launch site, where launch control and assembly of the balloon and its payload are conducted. The telemetry center is situated on a hill approximately 700 meters from the launch site. This is where balloon tracking, telemetry receiving, and radio commanding are conducted. In May 1987 a new telemetry center was constructed at the top of Mt. Ohkubo, 4.1 km. west of the launch site.

Ministry of International Trade and Industry (MITI). MITI promotes industrial utilization of space with particular regard to remote sensing and utilization of microgravity. Among the activities of MITI are the following:

- Development of observation systems of the Earth Resources Satellite;

- Development of the Advanced Spaceborne Thermal Emission and Reflection radiometer (ASTER), which is an advanced, multiband, high-resolution searching sensor to be mounted on NASA's Earth Observing System;

- Development of the Interferometric Monitor for Greenhouse gases, which will observe and monitor the distribution of rare elements in the atmosphere after being mounted on NASDA's Advanced Earth Observing Satellite;

- Research and development of technology facilities for utilizing remote sensing data;

- Participation in the Space Flyer Unit (SFU) project and promotion of microgravity experiments using SFU;

- Establishment of the System of Unmanned Reentry Capsule in cooperation with the German government and promotion of research and development using the system;
- Research and studies on space planes, space robots, and solar power satellites.

The Agency of Industrial Science and Technology (AIST), a branch of MITI, conducts studies in the space field through the following institutes:

- Electrotechnical Laboratory (ETL). ETL has conducted research on advanced technology for large-scale satellites. The main research area is space teleoperator, one aspect of space robotics. Another research topic is space power, including liquid droplet radiator and solar dynamic power systems. Material processing and remote sensing are also studied.
- Mechanical Engineering Laboratory (MEL). This institution is involved in work on mechanical systems such as attitude control systems for large space structures, model-based bilateral manipulation schemes, and fluid experiment systems in space.
- Geological Survey of Japan (GSJ). The function of GSJ is to promote geological applications in remote sensing such as establishing estimation techniques of silica content utilizing the mid-infrared spectra of minerals, rocks, and soils and developing extraction techniques for geologic interpretation using the visible and shortwave infrared imaging spectroscopy from space.

Ministry of Transport (MOT). The space-related organizations under MOT are Transport Policy Bureau as headquarters, the Electronic Navigation Research Institute as a subsidiary organization, and the Maritime Safety Agency and the Japan Meteorological Agency as affiliated entities. These organizations use meteorological, geodetic, and aeronautical satellites, and collect data from their use.

Recently, the importance of space technology development and its use in the transportation field has increased in such areas as meteorological and maritime observation, maritime geodetic control, Search and Rescue (SAR) in ships and aircraft, air traffic control, and operational control of ships, aircraft, and land vehicles. In addition, space technology, such as large-scale geostationary satellite expertise, has been steadily progressing.

Japan now believes that it would be much more economical and effective to launch a large, multipurpose satellite instead of launching several kinds of satellites separately in order to conduct meteorological observation and air traffic control. As a result of this thinking, the Ministry of Transport has been investigating the possibility of establishing a multipurpose satellite system to cover all the ministry's needs.

The ministry also supervises the National Space Development Agency of Japan (NASDA) in order to control satellite development. NASDA has been conducting a maritime geodetic survey to determine positions of the mainland and its off-lying islands as well as the distance between them with high accuracy using Japan's geodetic satellite "AJISAI" launched in August 1986.

High Frequency (HF) communications are presently used to control aircraft flying over the oceans. However, HF communication capacity is limited and tends to be unstable. Consequently, the Electronic Navigation Research Institute (ENRI) is now engaged in the research and development of a navigation and control system using satellites to improve significantly communication quality and surveillance capability for safety of transoceanic flights. The institute has been conducting navigation experiments on communications, positioning, and surveillance technology for the aircraft and ships using the Engineering Test Satellite-V launched in August 1987.

In order to establish the boundaries of Japanese territorial waters, the positions of the mainland and the off-lying islands must be registered with the World Geodetic System (WGS). The Maritime Safety Agency (MSA) has participated in the international joint observation plan, using the U.S. Laser Geodynamics Satellite since 1982 to fix the precise positions of Japanese territory based on the WGS.

The Japan Meteorological Agency (JMA) conducts space-based meteorological observations using geostationary meteorological satellites (GMS) and meteorological rockets as part of the World Weather Watch program of the World Meteorological Organization (WMO). The GMS observes cloud coverage and temperatures of sea surface and cloud top, and serves to collect the meteorological data from aircraft, buoys, and meteorological observation stations in remote areas.

As the ground facility to operate the GMS, the Japan Meteorological Agency has the Meteorological Satellite Center (MSC), which comprises the Data Processing Center (DPC) for the image data processing and the Command and Data Acquisition Station (CDAS) for the communication between the DPC and the GMS.

The data collected from satellites serve to improve weather forecasts on an operational basis, and are utilized in the International Satellite Cloud Climatology Project and the Global Precipitation Climatology Project of the WMO. The DPC also receives and analyzes data from the U.S. polar-orbiting meteorological satellites of NOAA.

Meteorological rockets observe temperature, atmospheric pressure, wind, and other phenomena at altitudes between thirty and sixty km. Launching of those rockets is carried out by the Meteorological Rocket

Observation Station, the only facility capable of meteorological rocket observation in the Far East and West Pacific region. The Meteorological Research Institute (MRI) is in charge of developing new techniques for more effective use of meteorological satellite data and conducts studies on sensors for the next generation of meteorological satellites.

Ministry of Posts and Telecommunications (MPT). MPT plans and promotes policy governing radio waves and space research and development related to the use of radio waves. The main activities of the ministry are: 1) research and development of long-range space communication concepts and complex satellite systems, and 2) research and development of a pilot plan for promoting satellite utilization and advanced satellite communication systems.

MPT has the Communications Research Laboratory (CRL) as an attached organization. It also supervises Nippon Telegraph and Telephone (NTT), Kokusai Denshin Denwa (KDD), Japan Broadcasting Corporation (NHK), the Telecommunications Satellite Corporation of Japan (TSCJ), and NASDA.

In addition to the agencies and institutes detailed above, the National Police Agency (police communications), the Geographical Survey Institute of the Ministry of Construction, and the Fire Defense Agency of the Home Affairs Ministry have made space-related budgetary appropriations.

International and Multilateral Cooperation

Japan's space activities to date have been promoted with emphasis on nonmilitary applications and international cooperation. Cooperation with the United States has been quite extensive. In the space station program, which is led by the United States with the participation of Canada, the European Space Agency, and Japan, Japan will provide the Pressurized Japan Experiment Module. Also, based on the agreement between the U.S. and the government of Japan in the field of space development of July 1969 and the Notes Verbale of December 1976 and December 1980, Japan has introduced U.S. equipment in several of its artificial satellites. Since January 1979 Japan has been receiving LANDSAT observation data about Japan and its vicinity.

Japan also cooperates with Europe in the field of space activities. In accordance with the agreement between Japan and ESRO, the predecessor of ESA, of December 1972, information and specialists are exchanged, and administrative-level meetings are held on a regular basis. At the administrative-level meetings, officials and specialists attend sessions of bodies on Earth observation, space transportation, and other topics. Japan is also conducting various studies and experiments with Germany in the fields of microgravity and space environments, under the Japan-German Technological Cooperation Agreement.

In 1981 when preparations for missions to encounter Halley's Comet were under way, four space agencies—Intercosmos of the then–Soviet Union Academy of Sciences, NASA of the U.S., the European Space Agency, and the Japanese Institute of Space and Astronautical Science (ISAS)—formed the Inter-Agency Consultative Group for Space Science (IACG). The task of IACG was to coordinate informally all matters related to the space missions to Halley's Comet and the observation of the comet from space. The collaboration under the IACG proved to be invaluable for the success of the cometary mission. Vital information was exchanged on the cometary path, the cometary dust environment, and related experiments. When the encounter ended all delegations recognized the advantage of such close cooperation, and agreed to continue the IACG. There are about twenty approved or planned missions scheduled to be completed between 1989 and 1996 under the auspices of IACG.

Japan has been active within the United Nations Committee on the Peaceful Uses of Outer Space and its Legal and Scientific Subcommittees since 1962.[78]

CANADA

On September 29, 1962, Canada's first scientific satellite, Alouette I, was launched. It was designed to provide information about the upper atmosphere to improve radio transmission on Earth. Designed to operate for a year, it lasted for an unprecedented ten years and earned Canada international recognition as the first nation after the United States and the Soviet Union to have a satellite in space.[79] Canada's mission in space is a practical way to fulfill a dream. Most of the Canadian space activities do not concern satellites and space ships, but the planet Earth and the real problems of people who live on it.[80]

The Canadian Space Agency Act was officially proclaimed by the governor general of Canada on December 14, 1990. Its mandate is to:

- promote the peaceful use and development of space;
- advance the knowledge of space through science; and
- ensure that space science and technology provide social and economic benefits for Canadians.[81]

The Canadian Space Agency brings together most of the existing space programs of the federal government. It coordinates all elements of Canada's space program and manages major space-related activities in Canada, although certain user-oriented programs have remained with other federal departments. A temporary headquarters was established in Montreal. At the same time, a high priority was given to establishing the agency's new headquarters in St. Hubert, which will physically unite its many functions and provide the most advanced facility for space work. Among the world's space agencies, the Canadian Space Agency ranks eighth in terms of government commitment per capita.

Canada's space program has long-standing ties to the U.S. National Aeronautics and Space Administration. The Canadian Space Agency's largest single project is its participation in the international space station Freedom. NASA is also a partner in Canada's RADARSAT program and its major partner in space science programs. Canada's international relations in space also feature its role as a cooperating member state in the European Space Agency. In 1989 a new ten-year cooperation agreement was reached with ESA. In 1989 a cooperation agreement was signed by the prime minister of Canada and the chairman of the Council of Ministers of the then–Soviet Union leading to active space cooperation. Also in 1989, the Canada-Japan Space Panel began studying ways to increase the ongoing space partnership between the two countries. Canada's other international partners in space include Sweden, Norway, France, and Brazil.

Remote Sensing. The value of international partnerships is clear in the field of Earth observation, where Canada participates in other countries' programs while receiving substantial support for RADARSAT. The RADARSAT program is also distinguished by the support it receives from other sources within Canada, including the private sector. Canada's RADARSAT is one of a new type of remote sensing satellites that is being developed in the 1990s.[82] Because it utilizes a Synthetic Aperture Radar sensor, RADARSAT is not restricted by cloud cover or darkness. It monitors land and sea conditions, providing Canada and the world with information needed for natural resource management, ice and ocean surveillance, and other applications. RADARSAT has attracted a wide range of partners. They include nine Canadian provinces, three Canadian space companies, and NASA and NOAA of the United States.

Space Station. By far the largest of all international space programs is the space station Freedom. Canada's involvement dates back to a 1988 agreement between the United States and Canadian governments. Canada's contribution to the space station is the Mobile Servicing System, the station's principal maintenance and payload handling system. It consists of two robots: the Space Station Remote Manipulating System and the Special Purpose Dextrous Manipulator. Canada occupies a strong position in the field of space robotics. The Strategic Technologies in Automation and Robotics Program (STEAR) aims to develop advanced strategic technologies for future upgrades of the Mobile Servicing System and to build the advanced industrial infrastructure necessary for Canada's continuing role in this area. The User Development Program (UDP) has been established to insure that Canadian industries, universities, and researchers take full advantage of the space station. UDP identifies areas of research in materials science and biotechnology with commercial potential.

In December 1990 the Canadian Space Agency was authorized to create a comprehensive Canadian space technology R&D capability and a contracting-out fund. The purpose of the fund is to build a strong space community throughout the country. The agency's internal Space Technology Program is based on the need to maintain a core competence within the agency in Canada's areas of space specialization. This includes research and development in space systems, robotics and automation, optical technologies, computer systems, dynamics and control of large space structures, materials for spacecraft, and thermal control. A Space Feasibility Fund was established to undertake cooperative feasibility studies of proposed space projects, including the Earth Environment Space Initiative.

Canada's space industry is the world's seventh largest in terms of revenue. It is one of the few that achieves greater revenues than funds spent by its own government. In the case of Canada's participation in the European Space Agency, for every dollar of Canadian government spending Canadian companies generate $3.50 of revenues. This achievement by Canadian industry reflects a well-established commercial market within Canada for space services, and well-regarded Canadian products that lead the world in their market niches. The viability of the space industry is also related to its success in finding new applications (spin-offs) of technology developed in the space program.[83]

AUSTRALIA

Australian institutions active in space research include the Commonwealth Scientific and Industrial Research Organization (CSIRO); numerous university groups; and various government bodies such as the Australian Center for Remote Sensing (ACRES), the Antarctic Division, the Bureau of Meteorology, the Bureau of Mineral Resources, and the Ionospheric Prediction Service.[84]

The Australian government announced its space policy in 1986, and established the Australian Space Board to oversee the national space program and to advise the minister for Industry, Technology, and Commerce. In September 1987 the Australian Space Office was formed within the Department of Industry, Technology, and Commerce to manage the national space program and to serve the Space Board. In September 1991 an expert panel was formed to assess the performance of the National Space Program. Among its proposals, there is one to strengthen the National Space Program by replacing the Australian Space Board with a statutory Australian Space Council, membership of which would include senior representatives of government agencies and people drawn from the industry and space science communities.

Australian space policy combines elements of both industry policy and science and technology policy. Government industry policy is aimed at developing internationally competitive, innovative industries, integrating Australian industry more closely into the world economy and reducing industry's reliance upon direct government assistance and regulation. The government's science and technology policy stresses the importance of science and technology for economic growth, the protection of the environment, and responsible uses of Australia's natural resources.

Recent activities of the Australian Space Office mainly focused on the implementation of the Space Industry Development Strategy, which provides the framework for the development of commercial space industry in Australia. The strategy is based upon the priority areas of satellite remote sensing, satellites for telecommunications, and space launch services.

In February 1992 the Remote Sensing Committee of the Space Board released a report that examines the role of remote sensing technology in a balanced national space program. The report, published by the Australian Space Office under the title "Observing Australia," gives particular emphasis to the identification of Australia's remote sensing data requirements over the next two decades. The Balanced National Space Program has introduced a broader dimension to the development of strategies for the expansion of Australia's space capabilities. An analysis of existing capabilities and future needs has suggested that satellite remote sensing will make an important contribution to meeting national requirements and assisting in the resolution of national problems. The Australian Space Office has therefore supported activities that encourage the translation of remote sensing science and technology to socially and economically beneficial applications for Australian and regional markets. It was recognized that provision of remote sensing image processing systems and training would broaden the exposure of Australia's technical capabilities to remote sensing operators from forty-two countries in the Asia-Pacific region.

Exchange of observers between the Committee on Remote Sensing and the Australian Liaison Committee on Remote Sensing by Satellite (AL-CORSS) to facilitate the provision of information among remote sensing organizations at the national level is still under way. The Space Office, in consultation with the Australian Center for Remote Sensing, also reestablished the Commonwealth Remote Sensing Committee to encourage discussion and consultation on remote sensing issues affecting commonwealth departments and agencies. The Space Office was a sponsor of the fifth Australasian Remote Sensing Conference in Perth in October 1990 and the Radar Remote Sensing Conference in Adelaide in April 1992.

There is a proposal to build a launch facility on Cape York. Initial development of the concept was undertaken by a consortium led by the Cape York Space Agency Pty Ltd. The concept involves a plan in which the company would purchase rockets from the former Soviet Union for use in an Australian commercial launch service that would operate in competition with existing launch services around the world. The proposed spaceport has the potential to offer significant economic benefits to Australia. Industry would also benefit: from construction and operation work at the spaceport itself, from industrial activity directly associated with the spaceport such as the manufacture of rocket fuel and components, and from spinoff industries and the consequent boost provided to space industry development.

In June 1991 the Space Board agreed to the establishment of three new Space Industry Development Centers (SIDCS) to complement the existing Australian Space Center for Signal Processing located at the University of South Australia. Introduced under the Infrastructure Development Program of the Australian Space Industry Development Strategy, the SIDC Program is a collaborative R&D activity aimed at promoting space-related R&D in order to develop Australian products and services capable of competing in international markets. The new centers are: a space industry development center for space engineering, a space industry development center in microwave technology, and a space center for satellite navigation technologies.

Under an intergovernment agreement between Australia and the United States, the Space Office is responsible for the management of the Canberra Deep Space Communication Complex (CDSCC) at Tidbinbilla, near Canberra, and the MOBLAS-5 satellite tracking laser at Yatharagga,

Western Australia, on behalf of the United States. CDSCC maintains a busy schedule of tracking operations. Regular communications are maintained with several NASA deep spacecraft and Earth-orbiting satellites.

In the space science field, the Upper Atmosphere and Cosmic Ray Physics programs have been combined in the Auroral and Space Physics department, and a strategic plan is being developed to monitor the atmosphere from the ground to the thermosphere. This program will focus on measurements of the dynamics of ozone in the stratosphere, temperatures and wind in the mesosphere, and winds and energy deposition in the thermosphere. These activities are being conducted in Antarctica because of the solar variability and the meteorological extreme cold temperatures in the Antarctic stratosphere and mesosphere. Other studies involve upper-atmosphere data collection, mesospheric and thermospheric dynamics, satellite signals, magnetic pulsation research, vertical electric field, and cosmic rays.

The Australian Surveying and Land Information Group (AUSLIG) is an Australian government agency providing commercial and public-interest land and geographic information services to government agencies, business, and the general public. AUSLIG's space-related activities include remote sensing and geodesy through its Australian Center for Remote Sensing (ACRES) and Geodesy Unit, respectively. ACRES comprises an operations element, outsourced from Computer Sciences of Australia (CSA), responsible for satellite data acquisition, processing and sales as a community service obligation activity, and an applications group undertaking projects and generating value-added products on a quasi-commercial basis.

The Australian Bureau of Meteorology operates an extensive real-time network for the reception and processing of remotely sensed data from meteorological and related satellites, and from radar. This network consists of facilities at Melbourne, Darwin, Perth, and Casey. The Remote Sensing Group of the Bureau of Mineral Resources' Geophysical Observatories and Mapping Program is involved in applications development of Earth-resources satellite data to support their National Geoscience Mapping Program. The bureau has been designated as a principal investigator of the European Space Agency for the evaluation of radar data from the ERS-1 spacecraft and its application for mapping materials in arid zone environments.

The Commonwealth Scientific and Industrial Research Organization (CSIRO) is Australia's largest research and development agency and comprises six research institutes, encompassing R&D in Information Science and Engineering; Natural Resources and Environment; Plant

Production and Processing; Mining, Energy and Construction; Industrial Technology; and Animal Production and Processing. Research is conducted in some thirty-six divisions, with approximately 100 laboratories throughout Australia and in a limited number of locations outside Australia.

INDIA

India is not a wealthy nation but, with a population of 850 million scattered over a surface of 1,266,595 square miles, it can hardly afford to neglect those space activities that can provide direct benefits to its development, such as telecommunications via satellite and remote sensing of the Earth.

India's space program is producing practical benefits that its politicians find difficult to oppose. Hundreds of millions of farmers living on the edge of subsistence need accurate data on soil and weather conditions. Land managers need to know the extent of forest loss so they can plant new trees to provide adequate fuel. A sprawling country with dozens of languages and a high rate of illiteracy desperately needs a communications system to tie together villages and cities.[85]

On a budget of less than $100 million a year, India manages to operate its own constellation of remote sensing and communication satellites, maintain numerous modern facilities, train engineers and scientists, and even conduct a small amount of space science. The Indian space industry has often been criticized by outsiders for being backward and rudimentary. But Western space powers should pay more attention to that industry in the future. With labor costs at an unbeatably low level and experience in building satellites on the rise, the Indians might someday become a commercial threat to their U.S. and European counterparts.

The principal Indian agency that deals with space activities is the Indian Space Research Organization (ISRO). Unlike NASA or the European Space Agency, ISRO assigns low priority to space science and advanced technology efforts. Instead, it is attempting to expand its network of communications and remote sensing satellites and develop a stable of launchers that will free the country from expensive reliance on U.S. and European space products.[86]

In addition to ISRO, India has several space facilities scattered throughout the country. There are five regional remote sensing centers and twenty-one remote sensing analysis centers founded by individual states, which focus mostly on local problems. In 1982 the National Natural Resources Management System was organized to link space officials with remote sensing data users. A planning committee composed of federal ministers gives the users a say in what data is needed for the future.

The Department of Space is responsible for operating a two-satellite system, a training program, and data analysis and interpretation. It spends almost $20 million per year on space applications, most of that on programs related to remote sensing. Federal ministries and state governments then fund their own efforts to use the information.[87] This cooperation has laid the groundwork for a new program called the National Resources Information System that combines federal, state, and local funding for a more coordinated approach to remote sensing use. The effort is to begin as an experimental five-year program tying together federal ministries, state governments, rural banks, and village leaders into a computer network that provides a comprehensive data base. Such a data base will combine remote sensing information with socioeconomic data such as population density and development needs.

India's philosophy of self-reliance is lately undergoing radical revisions. The new government is moving to ease restrictions on exports and imports, in an attempt to bring the country more fully into the global marketplace and spur faster development. The government recently accepted ISRO's proposal to start a new commercial company within the space agency, in an effort to bolster high-technology exports. The new company is part of a larger government effort to keep its well-trained engineers and scientists from immigrating to more developed countries and to expand the country's exports.

Chapter Two

The United Nations

The United Nations has been active in outer-space activities for over three decades through its own organs and departments and through the specialized agencies. The main divisions of the U.N. proper that deal with space activities are the following:

- Committee on the Peaceful Uses of Outer Space with its Legal Subcommittee and its Scientific and Technical Subcommittee;
- Outer Space Affairs Division;
- Department for Economic and Social Development;
- Center for Science and Technology for Development;
- Economic and Social Commission for Asia and the Pacific—The ESCAP Remote Sensing Program;
- Economic Commission for Africa—The African Regional Remote Sensing Program;
- Office of the United Nations Disaster Relief Coordinator;
- United Nations Environment Program;
- United Nations Development Program.

COMMITTEE ON THE PEACEFUL USES OF OUTER SPACE

The Committee on the Peaceful Uses of Outer Space (COPUOS) was established by the General Assembly in 1959, with a membership of twenty-four states, in order to promote international cooperation in the peaceful uses of outer space.[88] During the past thirty-three years the committee has compiled an impressive list of achievements and has established a framework of generally accepted principles that ensure that all countries can benefit from space activities. The international issues arising from space activities have grown steadily more complex over the years and the committee, which has expanded to fifty-three states, has adapted its agenda to deal with them.

The work of COPUOS and its member states has made outer space an exemplary field of international cooperation. The results of space research and development and the benefits of space applications have been made available to a large extent and are being widely used for social and economic development. Scientists and engineers from many countries are developing new technologies and applications for resource management, communications, weather and storm forecasting, environmental monitoring, and climate research. Though there are many bodies within the U.N. dealing with space activities, COPUOS has been designated by the General Assembly as the focal point for international cooperation in space, and it is the only body in the U.N. system with a mandate covering all aspects of the peaceful uses of outer space.

COPUOS provides an essential forum for guiding and coordinating the increasingly wide range of space activities handled by various divisions throughout the United Nations system. The Secretariat of the U.N., working under the committee's direction, emphasizes the coordination of space-related activities within the U.N. system. Within the Department of Political and Security Council Affairs the work of the Outer Space Affairs Division and its Program on Space Applications is coordinated through regular consultations with other agencies concerned with space activities to ensure that activities are not duplicated and that programs of common interest can be carried out jointly, making the most effective use of the limited resources available.

COPUOS has two standing subcommittees: the scientific and technical subcommittee and the legal subcommittee. The committee and its two subcommittees meet every year to consider questions put before them by the General Assembly, reports submitted to them, and issues raised by member states. The committee and its subcommittees, working on the basis of consensus, make recommendations to the General Assembly.

Legal Questions. As a result of the legal subcommittee's and COPUOS's work on legal issues associated with space activities, a number of treaties have been negotiated and concluded. They are:

- The Treaty on Principles Governing the Exploration and Use of Outer Space including the Moon and Other Celestial Bodies, which entered into force on October 10, 1968.
- The Agreement on the Rescue of Astronauts, Return of Astronauts, and the Return of Objects Launched into Outer Space, which entered into force on December 3, 1968.
- The Convention on International Liability for Damage Caused by Space Objects, which entered into force on September 1, 1972.
- The Convention on Registration of Objects Launched into Outer Space, which entered into force on September 15, 1976.
- The Agreement Governing the Activities of States on the Moon and Other Celestial Bodies, which entered into force in July of 1984.

During its thirty-first session, in 1992, the Legal subcommittee had three main items on its agenda.[89] They were the following:

- The Elaboration of Draft Principles Relevant to the Use of Nuclear Power Sources in Outer Space;
- Matters Relating to the Definition and Delimitation of Outer Space and to the Character and Utilization of the Geostationary Orbit, Including Consideration of Ways and Means to Ensure the Rational and Equitable Use of the Geostationary Orbit Without Prejudice to the Role of the International Telecommunication Union;
- Consideration of the Legal Aspects Related to the Application of the Principle that the Exploration and Utilization of Outer Space Should be Carried Out for the Benefit and Interests of All States, Taking into Particular Account the Needs of Developing Countries.

Other issues are still being debated and may not reach the agreement stage any time soon due to fundamental differences in both national interests of member states and political and philosophical approaches. On the other hand, with the incredible changes taking place in the 1990s, it is possible that some issues will be resolved due to a new commonality of views and interests among former adversaries.

Scientific and Technical Questions. The Scientific and Technical Subcommittee has been active and has made a series of recommendations on several subjects. Following are some of the most important issues.

Exchange of Information. The dissemination of information on the peaceful uses of outer space has been one of the primary concerns of COPUOS since its inception. Member states launching satellites and other space objects have been requested by the committee to provide the United

Nations with information on their launchings, for which a public registry was established by the secretary-general in March 1962. Since the Convention on Registrations of Objects Launched into Outer Space entered into force, another central register of objects has been established and information received from states and intergovernmental organizations that are parties to the convention.

Member states have also been urged to provide the committee with information on their national and cooperative international space programs. Information on these programs and activities has been issued in the annual review of national and cooperative international space programs.

Promotion of International Programs. One of the main purposes of establishing the committee was to study practical and feasible means of giving effect to programs in the peaceful uses of outer space that could appropriately be carried out under the auspices of the United Nations. To pursue this goal, the committee has taken steps to encourage international programs and scientific research projects such as the World Magnetic Survey and the International Indian Ocean Expedition.

In the area of practical applications of space technology, recommendations for international programs have been adopted in the field of space meteorology, space communications, navigation satellites, direct broadcasting by satellites, and remote sensing of the Earth by satellites.

COPUOS's concern with international cooperation in the application of space technology to meteorological programs and activities has been reflected in the recommendations to member states and to the World Meteorological Organization for measures designed to advance the state of atmospheric science and technology, with the goal of developing improved knowledge of basic physical forces affecting climate and the possibility of large-scale weather modification, and to improve weather forecasting capabilities.[90]

Promotion of Technical Cooperation in Specific Areas. Among the practical applications of specific concern to COPUOS are the fields of navigation satellites, remote sensing of the Earth by satellite, the use of nuclear power sources in space, the examination of the physical nature of the geostationary orbit, and space transportation systems.

The committee established in 1967 a Navigational Satellite Working Group and then endorsed the group's suggestion that the International Civil Aviation Organization (ICAO) and the Inter-Governmental Maritime Consultative Commission (now the International Maritime Organization, or IMO) as well as other specialized agencies should continue to study the requirements for potential applications for navigation services satellite systems in their area of competence. UNISPACE 82 also recognized the importance of position determination in real-time for navigation and called for the wide dissemination of computation techniques, equipment, and the information necessary for navigation and position-location using satellites. It also called for worldwide access to satellite navigation systems such as the United States Global Positioning System, a suggestion that has recently been accepted by the United States. The conference noted the importance of developing technologies and systems to enable smaller ships to use satellites for maritime communication and called on IN-MARSAT, along with ITU and IMO, to continue its efforts to develop smaller and less expensive ship terminals for communications, distress, and safety applications.

In the area of remote sensing, the Working Group on Remote Sensing concluded that useful applications of remote sensing data in the future might include the monitoring of the environment, studies in agriculture and forestry, geography, geology and mineral resources, hydrology and water resources, oceanography and marine resources, atmosphere, and meteorology. The working group also set out the alternatives and constraints on the ground segment (reception, distribution, storage, and interpretation of data) of the remote sensing systems.

In the field of direct broadcasting satellites the committee began discussions by setting up a working group in 1969 that convened for five sessions, until 1974. The working group reviewed some of the political and legal implications of direct broadcast satellites, and considered a number of issues for which the elaboration of principles in this field was considered essential. The working group was able to reach consensus on many draft principles. Other, unresolvable issues, were left to the legal subcommittee for further discussion.

The scientific and technical subcommittee established a Working Group on the Use of Nuclear Power Sources in Outer Space in 1979. The group was quick to realize that NPS could be very useful due to their long life, small size, and ability to operate without solar radiation but that both types of NPS, radio-isotope generators and nuclear reactors, required that appropriate design and operational measures be taken in order to protect the population and the environment for both normal and accidental conditions. In 1980 the working group focused on four items. First was the elaboration of an inventory of the safety problems involved in the use of NPS in space. Second, the working group discussed the application of recommendations of the International Commission on Radiological Protection (ICRP) for protection of populations and the environment relating to space vehicles utilizing NPS. The third item was the evaluation of existing methods in understanding orbital mechanics to determine whether improvements may be made in predicting reentry phenomena. The last item was the definition of technical considerations with regard to a format for notification. At its fifth session, in 1985, the working group dealt with the questions of emergency procedures and action plans in case of unplanned reentry of NPS.

Unispace 82 noted that the geostationary orbit is a natural resource of vital importance to a variety of space applications. It is, however, a limited resource and therefore requires optimal utilization through coordination and planning. The explosive growth in the use of the orbit, especially for communication satellites, has caused concern as to the availability of orbital positions and frequency assignments for countries that have not yet placed satellites into the orbit. At the root of COPUOS's concerns regarding the possible overcrowding of the geostationary orbit is the need to assure developing countries the right to position satellites on that orbit.

Questions relating to space transportation systems have been on the agenda of the Scientific and Technical Subcommittee since 1978. In 1979 the Secretariat, with the assistance of experts from the International Astronautical Federation (IAF), prepared a study on the international implications of new space transportation systems,[91] which was updated in 1981. [92]

Under the auspices of COPUOS, a variety of experiments have been conducted in order to study the nature of the space environment. In the early 1960s the committee considered the question of the potentially harmful effects of space experiments. UNISPACE 82 noted that the increase in the number of both space objects and launches created space debris. The conference concluded that the international community should agree upon appropriate measures for removing all inactive satellites from orbit. The conference also noted that pollution, radio disturbances, and the release of chemically reactive substances into space were a cause for increasing concern and that the disturbances in the ionosphere caused by the exhaust gases of rockets were a problem that needed study.

Within the United Nations system, UNESCO, ITU, and WMO have been directly and actively concerned with the applications of space technology, as well as aspects of the scientific exploration of outer space since the beginning of the space age. As space applications became more extensive in other fields, other organizations of the United Nations became increasingly involved in space programs and their ground applications. ICAO, IMO, the World Health Organization (WHO), the Food and Agriculture Organization of the United Nations (FAO), the International Labour Organization (ILO), the International Atomic Energy Agency (IAEA), and the World Bank have carefully followed space developments. To coordinate the activities of all these organizations and to work out joint programs, an Inter-Agency Meeting on Outer Space Activities meets annually and prepares a report that details activities planned for the future.

As an example of the latest activity of the Scientific and Technical Subcommittee of COPUOS, following is the agenda adopted at the meetings of the twenty-ninth session in 1992. [93]

- United Nations Program on Space Applications and the coordination of space activities within the United Nations system.
- Implementation of the recommendations of the Second United Nations Conference on the Exploration and Peaceful Uses of Outer Space.
- Matters relating to remote sensing of the Earth by satellites, including applications for developing countries.
- Use of nuclear power sources in outer space.
- Questions relating to space transportation systems and their implications for future activities in space.
- Examination of the physical nature and technical attributes of the geostationary orbit; examination of its utilization and applications including in the field of space communications, taking particular account of the needs and interests of developing countries.
- Matters relating to life sciences, including space medicine.
- Progress in national and international space activities related to the Earth environment, in particular progress in the geosphere-biosphere (global change) program.
- Matters relating to planetary exploration and astronomy.
- The theme fixed for special attention at the 1992 session of the Scientific and Technical Subcommittee: "Space technology and the protection of the Earth's environment: development of endogenous capabilities, in particular in the developing countries and in the context of the International Space Year."

OUTER SPACE AFFAIRS DIVISION

The division is part of the Department of Political and Security Council Affairs. It implements the decisions of the General Assembly and of the Committee on the Peaceful Uses of Outer Space.[94] It includes two sections: the Space Applications Section, which organizes and carries out the United Nations Program on Space Applications; and the Committee Services, Reports, and Research Section, which provides secretariat services to the committee, its scientific and technical subcommittee, and its subsidiary technical bodies. The division also assists the secretariat of the

Special Political Committee of the General Assembly during its consideration of outer space items.

As a result of the shifting emphasis from scientific exploration of outer space to the practical applications of space technology, the division has been increasingly involved in the implementation of the decisions of the committee and its subsidiary bodies to promote international cooperation in this field. In 1970 the secretary-general appointed an expert on space applications to the Outer Space Affairs Division. Among the recommendations of the expert was the adoption of a United Nations space applications program, which was begun in 1972. Under the auspices of the United Nations Space Applications Program, between 1972 and 1981 over 1,800 participants became involved in seminars, workshops, training courses, and panel meetings sponsored by the United Nations.

UNISPACE 82 recommended a number of new activities for the United Nations Space Applications Program including the following:

- promotion of greater exchange of actual experiences with specific applications;
- promotion of greater cooperation in space science and technology between developed and developing countries;
- organization of regular seminars on advanced space applications and new system developments for managers and leaders of space applications and technology development activities;
- stimulation of the growth of indigenous nuclei and an autonomous technological base in space technology, in developing countries with the cooperation of other U.N. agencies or member states;
- dissemination of information on new and advanced technology and applications, with emphasis on their relevance and implications for developing countries.

The division has also been active in promoting, through member states, fellowship programs for in-depth training. Individual countries have been requesting technical advisory services. Technical advisory missions have been carried out in a number of countries. As part of the program, the United Nations conducts three to four training courses annually on different aspects of space technology, including annual courses since 1976, cosponsored by FAO and the government of Italy, on remote sensing applications to various aspects of renewable resources. A new series of training courses on meteorology was started in 1983. These courses are being cosponsored by the United Nations, FAO, WMO, and the European Space Agency.

Another function of the division is to provide secretariat services to the Committee on the Peaceful Uses of Outer Space and its subsidiary bodies (except for the Legal Sub-Committee which is serviced by the Office of Legal Affairs of the United Nations) as well as to the secretariat of the Special Political Committee of the General Assembly when it considers space-related items. The studies that the division has undertaken for the committee range from background information to substantive studies in various areas of space research.

The secretary-general has administrative responsibilities under the major treaties on outer space that have been concluded under United Nations auspices. The division maintains an open registry containing information specified in article IV of the Registration Convention concerning objects launched into outer space. The division carries out, on behalf of the secretary-general, such functions as are entrusted to him under these treaties.

The Outer Space Affairs Division, in accordance with General Assembly resolution 1721 (XVI) of 1961, maintains regular contact with the specialized agencies concerned, in particular with ITU, WMO, UNESCO, FAO, and IMO. Representatives of the division often attend the meetings of those bodies when they relate to outer space activities.

DEPARTMENT FOR ECONOMIC AND SOCIAL DEVELOPMENT

The Department for Economic and Social Development (DESD) is in charge of a broad range of activities in the fields of cartography (surveying, mapping, and charting) geology, energy and mining, sea resources, and water resources. The department is basically divided into operational or field projects for technical assistance to developing countries and nonoperational activities including studies, seminars and conferences—also geared to meet the needs of developing countries.[95]

In the past, the department has been mostly interested in the application of satellite technology for geodesy, mapping, and earth resource surveys. In that connection, it participated in several United Nations conferences and seminars. More recently, cooperative activities of DESD have included projects to establish remote sensing centers in Mozambique, Poland, Ethiopia, and China and applications of remote sensing technologies for natural resource development in Ethiopia, Kenya, and Zaire. These projects focused on providing fellowships, technical assistance, and interpretation equipment.

Assistance has been provided to establish the Regional Remote Sensing Program (RRSP) for Asia and the Pacific region. DESD recruited the project manager and cooperates with the Economic and Social Commission for Asia and the Pacific as an Associated Executing Agency.

CENTER FOR SCIENCE AND TECHNOLOGY FOR DEVELOPMENT

The Center for Science and Technology for Development was established pursuant to General Assembly resolution 34/218 of 1979, as an organizationally distinct entity within the United Nations Secretariat.[96] The work of the center is reviewed by the Intergovernmental Committee on Science and Technology for Development (IGCSTD), which was established under the same resolution. It is a committee of the whole and submits its report and recommendations to the General Assembly through the Economic and Social Council.

The center assists the director-general for Development and International Co-operation in fulfilling the responsibilities entrusted to him by the Vienna Program of Action on Science and Technology for Development. It provides important support to IGCSTD as well as to its subsidiary body, the Advisory Committee for Science and Technology for Development (ACSTD), which reports to IGCSTD and through it provides expert advice to the General Assembly, the Economic and Social Council, and other bodies of the United Nations. The center closely cooperates with state members of IGCSTD as well as with other organs of the U.N. system, particularly through the joint interagency Task Force on Science and Technology for Development established by the Administrative Committee on Co-ordination (ACC).

The center does not provide technical assistance to developing countries on an operational basis, but it has been and is involved in a number of ways in space activities. For example, the center has undertaken activities aimed at establishing an international mechanism for the early identification and assessment of space development implications. Three major components were proposed for the Advance Technology Alert System: a semiannual bulletin, the provision of advice and assistance to member states, and the establishment of a network of research institutes.

In order to implement the Vienna Program of Action, the ACC Task Force on Science and Technology formulated twenty-four joint activities with the designation of lead agencies and participating organizations and a definition of their roles. These twenty-four activities include a project on interregional assessment and strengthening of remote sensing applications technology in developing countries, with FAO as the lead agency and ten other participating organizations of the U.N. system.

UNITED NATIONS DEVELOPMENT PROGRAM

The UNDP administers and coordinates the great majority of the technical assistance provided through the U.N. system. Its objective is to assist developing countries in accelerating their economic and social development by providing regular and sustained assistance geared to their development needs, with the aim of promoting their economic and political independence and ensuring the attainment of higher levels of economic and social development for their populations.

The UNDP began operations in 1966 as a result of General Assembly resolution 2029 (XX), which combined the U.N. Expanded Program of Technical Assistance (EPTA) with the Special Fund. Assembly resolution 2688 (XXV) of 1971 defined the present organizational structure and activities of the UNDP. The special fund and the technical assistance components of the program were completely merged and the Governing Council commenced consideration of integrated country programs. Most of the projects funded by the program are executed by agencies and organizations within the U.N. system.[97]

The program has funded projects in the areas of satellite broadcasting, satellites in telecommunication, remote sensing, aerial photography, and aerial surveys.

UNITED NATIONS ENVIRONMENT PROGRAM

UNEP was established pursuant to General Assembly resolution 94 (XXVII) of 1972. In resolution 2997 (XXVII) the assembly established a governing Council for Environmental Programs.

The main interest of UNEP in outer space activities is in remote sensing as an important tool for systematically collecting data on environmental variables. This data collection is carried out by the Global Environmental Monitoring System (GEMS), which is coordinated by the UNEP Program Activity Center on GEMS. GEMS itself is a concerted effort on the part of member states, UNEP, FAO, WHO, WMO, and other United Nations agencies to ensure that relevant data are collected in an orderly and adequate manner in order to obtain a quantitative picture of the state of the environment and of the natural and man-made regional and global trends undergone by critical environmental variables.[98]

The GEMS and Regional Seas Program Activity Centers of UNEP consider remote sensing techniques for use in detecting and monitoring marine pollutants. Satellite data is also used for mapping mangrove forests and monitoring the impact of pollutants on them. In Latin America and southwest Asia UNEP is developing transnational programs to monitor desertification processes and related natural resources. Each project is supported by the government concerned, together with one or more external donors. All projects have a large remote sensing component.

The GEMS tropical forest resource assessment, an ongoing joint UNEP/FAO effort that makes heavy use of satellite data, has been expanded to temperate regions as well. Assessment data are now the basis of a GEMS forest resource data base (FORIS) at FAO. Methods are being developed for Advanced Very High Resolution Radiometer data provided by the NOAA series of meteorological satellites.

In cooperation with NASA of the United States, the GEMS Program Activity Center is developing programs to use NOAA-satellite data to monitor global changes in land surface state, vegetation cover, and land use.

UNEP is supporting the International Association of Meteorology and Atmospheric Physics in the development of an implementation plan for an International Satellite Land-surface Climatology Project. It has also established software and hardware criteria for the planned Global Resource Information Database, a project that is now being implemented with GEMS.

OFFICE OF THE UNITED NATIONS DISASTER RELIEF COORDINATOR

By resolution 2816 (XXVI) of 1971, the General Assembly authorized the establishment of a permanent office in Geneva to be the focal point for disaster relief, preparedness and prevention in the U.N. system, headed by a disaster relief coordinator who reports directly to the secretary-general.

In conjunction with the National Center for Space Studies (CNES) in Toulouse, France, UNDRO has since 1983 conducted a series of field trials of a portable satellite transmitter, using ARGOS/COSPAS satellite systems. The transmitter, provided by CNES, contains a keyboard that allows an UNDRO relief officer on site to enter detailed information about a disaster and the priority relief requirements and to transmit this information automatically to UNDRO in Geneva.[99] In 1984 the United Nations concluded an agreement with INTELSAT, permitting the use of INTEL-SAT satellites for both peace-keeping and disaster relief operations.

Since 1981 the Satellite Weather Bulletin Service of the National Ocean and Atmospheric Administration of the United States has been installed at UNDRO, provided through the World Weather Watch program of WMO. The system provides notification of tropical cyclones. The messages give satellite-derived positions and intensity estimates of the storms. The reports are transmitted twice a day for active storms and are based on information derived by NOAA. Also, UNDRO receives regular alerts from FAO for early warnings of developing food shortages.

UNDRO cooperates with FAO and ESA in holding regular training courses for officials from disaster-prone developing countries in the use of space technology for disaster prevention and preparedness work.

Earth observation from satellites may be used in disaster prevention in two ways: in producing hazard risk maps and, to a limited extent, in the mapping of crop types. These data can be used to assess the effectiveness of current crop practices, thus providing the data needed to formulate advisory strategies for the improvement of these practices and limit the effects of drought and other catastrophic climatic conditions.[100] Earth observation by satellites can also be used to map flood plains and delineate the areas of potential flood impact. On occasion, satellite observation can provide information on surface cover changes in watersheds and this can become a key factor in plans for flood prevention and preparedness, including watershed management and engineering works.

ECONOMIC AND SOCIAL COMMISSION FOR ASIA AND THE PACIFIC

ESCAP Regional Remote Sensing Program

The Economic Commission for Asia and the Far East was established by Economic and Social Council Resolution 37 (IV) of 1947. In 1974, by resolution 1895 (LVII) ECOSOC approved the change of name to the Economic and Social Commission for Asia and the Pacific.

The work of ESCAP is conducted through the annual sessions and through meetings of the main legislative committees and subsidiary bodies. There are currently seven legislative committees.

The objectives of the Remote Sensing Program include provision of seminars, training courses, workshops and establishment of a regional information service including promotion of regional joint research projects or pilot application projects. The RRSP began in March 1983 and is housed in the Natural Resources Division of ESCAP. The funds for the program are provided by UNDP. ESCAP is the executing agency, and FAO and TCD are associate executing agencies.

The program is managed by a project manager/coordinator who is assisted by an expert on remote sensing and by two administrative staff.

In order to give the program policy guidance and advice, an Intergovernmental Consultative Committee on the RRSP has been established by the governments of China, Indonesia, Malaysia, Nepal, the Philippines, Singapore, Sri Lanka, and Thailand. Other countries have joined later.

ECONOMIC COMMISSION FOR AFRICA

African Regional Remote Sensing Program

The Economic Commission for Africa (ECA) was established by ECOSOC resolution 671 (XXV) of 1958 to initiate and participate in measures for facilitating concerted action for the economic development of Africa with a view to raising the level of economic activity and living standards in Africa. The commission meets annually.

The African Regional Remote Sensing Program (ARSP) is a regional cooperation program established in 1975 to make remote sensing techniques available to all state members of ECA for resource development and effective monitoring of environmental changes.

The objectives of the program are to serve as a machinery for the implementation of a comprehensive remote sensing policy for its member states, to ensure that all the advantages of remote sensing technology are accessible to all the member states, and to foster close cooperation among African nations in matters relating to remote sensing.

The Cartography and Remote Sensing Unit in the Natural Resources Division of the Secretariat is charged with responsibility for the implementation of ARSP. Two other units in the secretariat, namely, the Communications Unit in the Transport, Communications, and Tourism Division and the Environmental Unit in the Social Development and Human Settlements Division, are also involved in space technology applications. Their activities are concerned with the applications of space technology to communications and the environment.[101]

ARSP is implemented by the following organs: the African Remote Sensing Council (the principal organ) and other subsidiary organs including the Governing Board, the Technical Advisory Committee, the Regional Management Committees, and the Regional Remote Sensing Centers. The work program of the ECA secretariat includes technical advisory services to member states to make them aware of the potential of remote sensing applications to their resource development.

Chapter Three

Specialized Agencies of the United Nations

FOOD AND AGRICULTURE ORGANIZATION OF THE UNITED NATIONS

Remote Sensing Center

FAO was established in 1945 when forty-four governments indicated acceptance of the constitution drafted by an interim commission. The preamble of the constitution defines the aim of the members as being "to promote the common welfare by furthering separate and collective action . . . for the purposes of raising levels of nutrition and standards of living of the peoples under their respective jurisdictions, securing improvements in the efficiency of the production and distribution of all food and agricultural products, bettering the conditions of rural populations, and thus contributing toward an expanding world economy."

In 1980, at the request of the Committee on the Peaceful Uses of Outer Space, FAO established a Remote Sensing Center to cover, within the U.N. system, remote sensing applications to renewable natural resources. The center, in consultation with FAO technical divisions, acts as the focal point for activities in space applications, particularly for aspects of agriculture, fisheries, and forestry. It provides technical assistance to a large number of field projects using remote sensing and is closely involved in the formulation and execution of regular program activities with a remote sensing component, including a range of activities carried out in collaboration with other United Nations Agencies.[102]

The Remote Sensing Center, located at FAO headquarters in Rome, includes the following technical support facilities:

- A geographic data base of satellite imagery;
- A remote sensing reference library;
- A primary data user station for real-time reception of Meteosat data;
- A laboratory for analogue interpretation of aerial photographs and analog and digital analysis of environmental and Earth resources satellite imagery;
- Photogrammetric equipment for small-scale thematic mapping and cartography;
- Photographic facilities for producing prints and transparencies;
- Access to an expanding international telecommunication network of remote sensing databases.

The center conducts a range of training activities both in host countries for courses at the national and regional levels, and at headquarters for courses at the interregional level. It also advises and assists developing countries on the applications of remote sensing and the development of their programs and facilities. The center represents FAO in several bodies within the U.N. system and on international and major national bodies concerned with space applications.

Many projects currently being operated by FAO include applications of remote sensing. For the most part this involves the use of black-and-white aerial panchromatic photographs, color and color infrared aerial photographs, and Landsat data, both as prints of multispectral imagery for field use and as obtained by interactive computer-assisted techniques.

The regional monitoring of vegetation change and the monitoring of agricultural drought provide important inputs to the FAO Early Warning System on Food Security. Activities relating to fisheries include the preparation of a manual on the applications of remote sensing to marine fisheries and an exercise to demonstrate the use of satellite remote sensing for aquaculture site selection. In the area of forestry, FAO activities consist of projects to monitor deforestation, reforestation, national parks, and national forests. The Tropical Forest Cover Monitoring Program in Brazil is the world's largest.

FAO is regularly represented at the meetings of the United Nations Committee on the Peaceful Uses of Outer Space and its Scientific and Technical Subcommittee, and at the United Nations Inter-Agency meetings on outer space activities. Close contact is maintained with the United Nations Outer Space Affairs Division, with which several joint training programs for developing countries have been carried out. Collaboration continues to be expanded with regional and national centers concerned with satellite data acquisition, data processing, and distribution of imagery to users. There has also been cooperation with WMO in the form of joint training courses in agrometeorology.

The center maintains close contact with the Canada Center for Remote Sensing, CNES, and the Group for the Development of Aerospace Remote Sensing (GDTA) in France, the National Space Research Commission in Argentina, the German Aerospace Research Establishment (DFVLR), INPE in Brazil, ESA, the National Aeronautics and Space Council (NASC) in the United Kingdom, the National Remote Sensing Agency in India, the National Remote Sensing Center in China, the Remote Sensing Technology Center in Japan, and Telespazio in Italy. In the United States, the Remote Sensing Center has frequent contacts with NASA, which supplies FAO with NOAA AVHRR vegetation index color composites, and with NOAA, which provides microfiches of Tiros-N data.

FAO also cooperates with various governmental and international scientific bodies concerned with remote sensing research. It is also closely associated with the International Union of Forest Research Organizations.

UNITED NATIONS EDUCATIONAL, SCIENTIFIC, AND CULTURAL ORGANIZATION (UNESCO)

UNESCO was established in 1945 to promote the aims set forth in its charter. The purpose of UNESCO, as stated in article 1 of said charter, is: "to contribute to peace and security by promoting collaboration among the nations through education, science and culture in order to further universal respect for justice, for the rule of law, and for the human rights and fundamental freedoms which are affirmed for the peoples of the world, without distinction of race, sex, language or religion, by the Charter of the United Nations."

Within UNESCO, the use of satellites for communications is dealt with by two divisions in the Sector for Communication.[103] First, the Division of Development of Means of Communication is concerned with feasibility studies, training and production of appropriate low-cost broadcasting equipment relating to communication satellites. The Division of Free Flow of Information and Communication Policies is responsible for all aspects of international exchange of information and television news and programs via communication satellites. In addition, the International Program for the Development of Communication, which was created in 1980 by the General Conference of UNESCO, examines and supports projects for the utilization of communication satellites within and between countries.

UNESCO promotes international arrangements and conventions in close cooperation with the Office of International Norms and Legal Affairs. It assists member states, principally in the form of missions to provide expert advice on the use of space communication for education and national development, with the support of the Division of Methods, Materials, and Techniques in the Education Sector.

UNESCO's interests in remote sensing of the Earth by satellites and other spacecraft are mostly connected with studies of the natural environment and its resources. The use of space remote sensing, together with conventional (airborne) remote sensing techniques, is handled by the following units of the UNESCO Science Sector:

- Division of Ecological Sciences
- Division of Earth Sciences
- Division of Water Sciences
- Division of Marine Sciences
- Secretariat of the Intergovernmental Oceanographic Commission.

The involvement of UNESCO in space activities is mostly concentrated on remote sensing techniques, particularly their application in international research, their use in environmental monitoring, and their diffusion in developing countries. UNESCO provides expert services and surveys in the areas of geology and related fields. In the field of marine sciences, UNESCO has been involved in a remote sensing component for a marine science center in Iran. In the framework of the World Climate Research Program (WCRP), UNESCO has been involved in two major experiments designed by the Scientific Committee on Oceanic Research, Committee on Climate Changes and the Ocean.

In the field of communications, UNESCO provides expert services on all questions related to the use of satellites for broadcasting services and for the transmission of news agency material. The International Program for the Development of Communication provides additional contributions.

Cooperation with the United Nations, ITU, and other members of the U.N. system has marked every stage of the development of UNESCO programs. The director-general of UNESCO has been represented at relevant meetings of the United Nations and ITU. UNESCO also participates regularly in the meetings of the Scientific and Technical Subcommittee of COPUOS, as well as in conferences and seminars of nongovernmental organizations.

INTERNATIONAL CIVIL AVIATION ORGANIZATION

ICAO came into existence on April 4, 1947, after twenty-six states had ratified the convention signed at Chicago in 1944. Article 44 of the convention assigns to ICAO the functions of developing the principles and techniques of international air navigation and fostering the planning and development of international air transport so as to ensure the safe and orderly growth of international civil aviation throughout the world. As of 1990 the organization had 160 members.

The interests of ICAO in space affairs are governed by its supreme organ, the Assembly, which in 1977 adopted the following resolution A22-20:

1. "RESOLVES that ICAO be responsible for stating the position of international civil aviation on all related outer space matters;
2. URGES that Contracting States continue keeping the Organization informed regarding the programmes and the progress achieved in the exploration and use of outer space that are of interest to international civil aviation;
3. REQUESTS the Council to continue its work with regard to the planning and use of space technology for air navigation, and to take steps aimed at an active continuation of the work of determining the operational and technical requirements for an international satellite system for air navigation, taking due account of economic considerations, as well as of the provisions of resolution A22-18, appendix J, regarding the co-ordination of aeronautical systems and sub-systems;
4. REQUESTS the Secretary-General to ensure that the International Civil Aviation positions and requirements are made known to all organizations dealing with relevant space activities and to continue to arrange for the Organization to be represented at appropriate conferences and meetings connected with or affecting the particular interests of international civil aviation in this field."

The ICAO Governing Council is made up of representatives of thirty-three States elected by the Assembly. The Air Navigation Committee is made up of fifteen technical experts elected by the council from nominations made by contracting states and advises the Council on the air navigation aspects of space technology. In 1968 the Air Navigation Commission established a panel of experts, the Application of Space

Techniques Relating to Aviation (ASTRA) Panel, to pursue the technical interests of international civil aviation in space applications.[104]

WORLD HEALTH ORGANIZATION

Article 1 of the WHO constitution, which was adopted in 1946,[105] defined the organization's objective as "the attainment by all peoples of the highest possible level of health."

WHO endeavors to keep abreast of developments in space research since the results of such research may have a bearing on certain of its programs, particularly when they relate to the relationship with the environment. The main areas of interest to WHO are: environmental health, epidemiology and communication sciences, occupational health, cardiovascular diseases, radiation health, nutrition, mental health, human genetics, and the organization of medical care.

Particular areas to which space activities are relevant include techniques for determining vector habitats in relation to malaria and other diseases. Remote sensing techniques can be valuable in identifying regions of high water pollution and oil spills.[106] Other water-quality parameters potentially measurable with remote sensing techniques include turbidity and salinity. Studies in the field of air pollution have also been conducted. Remote sensing of the atmosphere has made it possible to detect such pollutants as carbon monoxide, sulfur dioxide, oxides of nitrogen, carbon dioxide, and particulates.

WHO has also been interested in remote sensing applications to forestry and agriculture because of the potential use of such technology in detecting potential breeding and resting sites of vectors of major importance.

WHO has close relations with the various organizations concerned with space studies. It has cooperated with IAF and the International Academy of Astronautics (IAA) and has sent a four-member mission to NASA in order to draw up an inventory of present possibilities and future prospects offered by space technology.

WORLD BANK (INTERNATIONAL BANK FOR RECONSTRUCTION AND DEVELOPMENT)

The International Bank for Reconstruction and Development (IBRD) came into being at the 1944 Bretton Woods Conference and began operation in 1946–1947. It was established to promote the international flow of capital for productive purposes and to assist in financing of nations destroyed by World War II. Lending for productive projects or to finance reform programs that will lead to economic growth in its less developed member countries is now the bank's main objective.

In line with its current objectives, the bank is interested in the peaceful uses of outer space, and how developments in this field might contribute to the development process in the bank's developing member countries. Its particular interest lies in satellite data analysis, education and telecommunications.

Two sections within the bank deal with satellite imagery: the Economics and Resource Division of the Agriculture and Rural Development Department and the Cartographic Section of Administrative Services. The Education Projects Department retains the services of a mass media specialist to assist the governments of developing countries in formulating plans for using communication media, including satellites, to upgrade and expand education.[107]

The Economic and Resource Division is engaged in a variety of analytical work based on satellite data in computer tape form, while the Cartographic Section deals primarily with the film products and applications derived from those products. This work is carried out in connection with bank-financed projects in its developing member countries.

The activities of the bank in space telecommunications have concentrated on financing a number of Earth stations for domestic and international communications via satellite. Both large, type-A stations and smaller terminals have been included.

The bank keeps in touch with the latest developments in space applications and closely cooperates with many national and international organizations, especially those within the U.N. system.

INTERNATIONAL TELECOMMUNICATION UNION

The ITU, founded in 1865, held its thirteenth plenipotentiary conference at Nice in 1989. The constitution signed at that meeting came into force on January 1, 1990. The fourteenth conference will be held in Tokyo in 1994. The purposes of the Union are:

- to maintain and extend international cooperation between all members of the union for the improvement and rational use of telecommunications of all kinds, as well as to promote and to offer technical assistance to developing countries in the field of telecommunications;

- to promote the development of technical facilities and their most efficient operation with a view to improving the efficiency of telecommunication services, increasing their usefulness and making them, so far as possible, generally available to the public;

- to promote the use of telecommunication services with the objective of facilitating peaceful relations;
- to harmonize the actions of nations in the attainment of those ends.

ITU's structure can be summarized as follows:

1. Plenipotentiary Conference, which is the supreme organ of the union;
2. Administrative Conferences;
3. Administrative Council;
4. Permanent organs of the union, which are:

   - General Secretariat;
   - International Frequency Registration Board (IFRB);
   - International Radio Consultative Committee (CCIR);
   - International Telegraph and Telephone Consultative Committee (CCITT);
   - Telecommunications Development Bureau (BDT).

A large part of the work of ITU is related to the preparation and servicing of administrative radio conferences, at which are established the technical criteria and regulatory procedures to govern the use of frequency bands and radiocommunication services. Another important function of the union arises from the need to carry out the tasks given to it by the administrative conferences, which may include enforcement (without sanction) of regulatory procedures, technical studies related to the establishment of telecommunication systems, and technical studies of frequency-sharing by different services.

Another significant effort of ITU is its technical assistance to developing countries which generally covers three areas:

- education, which includes professional training;
- support of individual satellite projects;
- development of general plans for telecommunication systems.

The uses of telecommunications in space systems fall into two categories:[108]

1. The first category includes satellites, the function of which is to provide telecommunication links between points on the Earth's surface, or to broadcast to the public in general;

2. The second category includes all space vehicles, manned or unmanned, used for space research, Earth observation, planetary exploration, manned scientific missions, or others in which the radiocommunications subsystem is secondary to the primary mission. Here the radio links are for the purpose of transmitting the collected data from the space vehicle to a receiving terminal.

In both categories the same physical phenomena are involved in radiocommunications. Thus many of the problems, in particular the choice of frequency, can be of a regulatory nature. The technical study and regulatory work of ITU with respect to space telecommunications relates to both categories in the sense that it seeks to ensure an interference-free environment for the vital radiocommunication links for all space missions.

The radio regulations give extensive tasks to IFRB in the areas of disseminating the technical information concerning new satellite systems. With the increasing utilization of the geostationary orbit, it became clear that the tasks cannot be accomplished without the existence of an extensive computer database.

The IFRB has been working on the establishment of an extensive database management system for the frequency management tasks that are required at the international level. The database should contain all the pertinent information concerning radiocommunication frequency usage that is received from governments and will have application programs to permit the assessment of potential radio interference situations.

Among the CCIR study groups of interest to space activities are the following:

- Study Group 2—space research and radioastronomy services;
- Study Group 4—fixed-satellite service;
- Study Group 8—mobile, radio-determination and amateur services;
- Study Groups 10 and 11—broadcasting satellite service.

WORLD METEOROLOGICAL ORGANIZATION

The WMO, successor to the International Meteorological Organization that had been established in 1873, formally came into existence in 1950. The basic functions of the organization are to:

- Facilitate international cooperation in the establishment of networks of stations to provide meteorological and related services;

- Promote the establishment and maintenance of systems for rapid exchange of meteorological and related information;
- Promote standardization of meteorological and related observations to ensure the uniform publication of observations and statistics;
- Further the application of meteorology to aviation, shipping, water problems, agriculture, and other human activities;
- Encourage research and training in meteorology.

WMO is composed of the following organs:

1. World Meteorological Congress;
2. Executive Council;
3. Six regional meteorological associations;
4. Eight technical commissions;
5. Secretariat.

The advent of Earth satellites continues to have considerable impact on the activities of WMO and to provide great benefits to meteorological and operational hydrological services throughout the world. Practically all of the constituent bodies of WMO are engaged, directly or indirectly, in satellite-related activities.[109]

The activities of WMO relating to outer space come under the following major programs of the organization.

1. *World Weather Watch Program*—WWW is a worldwide system composed of the co-ordinated facilities and services provided by the members of WMO and supplemented by international organizations. In accordance with the WWW Plan and Implementation Program, meteorological satellites constitute the space-based subsystem of the Global Observing System, to supplement the information provided by the ground-based subsystems in order to complete the global coverage. Current meteorological satellites are of two types: near polar-orbiting satellites and geostationary meteorological satellites. To a large extent, the two types of meteorological satellites are complementary. The geostationary satellites provide almost continuous measurements and surveillance in tropical and temperate latitudes, while the near polar-orbiting satellites perform functions at higher latitudes and over polar regions.

2. *World Climate Program*—The WMO Congress of 1979 decided that the WCP should comprise the following four components:

   - World Climate Applications Program (WCAP);
   - World Climate Data Program (WCDP);

- World Climate Research Program (WCRP);

- World Climate Impacts Program (WCIP).

WMO has responsibility for the first two components. The World Climate Research Program is a joint program between WMO and ICSU. UNEP has the primary responsibility for the fourth program.

WCAP—The Commission for Climatology is concerned, among other things, with the development and improvement of methodologies for the application of meteorological (especially climatological) information in such fields as energy, engineering and building, land use and human settlements, tourism, industry, transportation, communications, and economic and social planning. The commission has a rapporteur on the use of meteorological data obtained by remote sensing.

WCDP—The purpose of this program is to ensure timely access to reliable climate data that can be exchanged in acceptable format to support climate applications, impact studies, and research. The scope of WCDP includes climate data from the entire climate system, including the atmosphere, oceans, cryosphere, and land surface. Climate system monitoring for WCDP, using satellite-derived data, is carried out by WMO, in cooperation with UNEP, as a GEMS activity.

WCRP—The main objectives of this program are to determine the extent to which climate can be predicted and the extent of human influence on climate. The basic approach focuses on the use of physical-mathematical models for simulating and predicting climate changes over a wide range of space and time scales.

3. *Research and Development Program*—In carrying out the program, the following areas have been defined as highest priority for promoting WMO members' activities: short and medium-range weather prediction research, long-range forecasting research, tropical meteorology, environmental pollution monitoring, and research on weather modification and climate.

4. *Application of Meteorology Program*

   a) Agricultural Meteorology Program—The WMO Commission for Agricultural Meteorology (CAgM) has long been concerned with the application of remote sensing techniques to agrometeorological research and applications. Present programs include compilation of practical satellite applications to agrometeorology, guidance material on aspects of satellite applications to agrometeorology, and training courses on that subject. One of the main objectives of CAgM is to provide members with practical guidance on satellite data that can be used in agriculture, forestry and the fight against desertification.

   b) Aeronautical Meteorology Program—This program is planned and developed within WMO by the Commission for Aeronautical Meteorology (CAeM). It takes into account the operational requirements expressed by ICAO. Close cooperation is maintained with other international organizations, in particular with the International Air Transport Association (IATA), the International Council of Aircraft Owner and Pilot Associations, and the International Federation of Air Line Pilots Associations. The space-related activities conducted under the program include the use of satellite data for preparation of information required for flight operation, the direct use of satellite imagery and other satellite data for short-range weather forecasting, and satellite support to the World Area Forecast System (WAFS).

c) Marine Meteorology Program—This program, the Integrated Global Ocean Services System (IGOSS), and other ocean-related activities are planned and conducted within WMO by the Commission for Marine Meteorology and the Joint IOC/WMO Working Committee for IGOSS. Under the program, space activities occur in two areas: the use of satellite sensors to measure several meteorological and oceanographic parameters at the air-sea interface including sea-surface temperature, sea ice, surface winds, ocean waves, etc.; and the use of satellites in marine telecommunications for the collection of meteorological data from ships and ocean buoys and for the distribution of meteorological service products to ships.

5. *Hydrology and Water Resources Program*—The WMO Commission for Hydrology is responsible for the development and use of applications of space technology to hydrology. Among the projects undertaken in this program are the following:

- Technical reports on remote sensing techniques and multisensor data analysis in operational hydrology and on applications of satellite data for estimation of precipitation;

- A technical report on snow-cover measurement and aerial assessment of precipitation and soil moisture;

- A study on the estimation of spatial and temporal variations of soil water content and the water content of the atmosphere by remote sensing techniques;

- A study of the role of remote sensing and transmission capabilities of satellites in hydrological network design.

INTERNATIONAL MARITIME ORGANIZATION

The Convention on the International Maritime Organization (IMO), concluded at Geneva in 1948, came into force in 1958. The organization's main purpose is to facilitate cooperation among governments on technical matters affecting international shipping, in order to achieve the highest practicable standards of maritime safety and efficiency in navigation.

Since 1966 IMO has taken part in the development and application of satellite technology at sea. The units dealing with space activities within

IMO are the Assembly, the Council, and the Maritime Safety Committee, as well as its subcommittees on radiocommunications and on safety of navigation.

Given the potential contribution of satellites to maritime distress and safety systems and to maritime communications, IMO submitted a report from the maritime perspective on the use of space technology to the 1971 WARC on Space Telecommunications organized by ITU. Following that conference, the Maritime Safety Committee initiated the preparation of a plan for establishing an international maritime satellite system. IMO convened an International Conference on the Establishment of an International Maritime Satellite System. At the third session, the conference adopted the Convention on the International Maritime Satellite Organization (INMARSAT), which came into force in 1979.[110]

Chapter Four

Nongovernmental Institutions

INTERNATIONAL COUNCIL OF SCIENTIFIC UNIONS

ICSU was established in 1931 to succeed the International Research Council (founded in 1919), to provide a central body through which the world scientific community could encourage international scientific cooperation.[111] Membership is composed of two categories: international scientific unions and academies and research councils. The scientific members are the adhering scientific unions, each representing one branch of science. The national members are the national academies of science, national research councils or equivalent bodies of the countries adhering to the council.

The objectives of the council are:

- to encourage international scientific activity;
- to facilitate and coordinate the activities of the international scientific unions;
- to stimulate, design, and coordinate international interdisciplinary scientific research projects and scientific education;
- to facilitate the coordination of the international scientific activities of its national members.

To carry out the above objectives, the council may enter into relations with governments of member countries and maintain relations with the United Nations or other international intergovernmental or nongovernmental organizations.

ICSU first became involved in space activities by developing the International Geophysical Year program of 1957. In 1958 ICSU created the Committee on Space Research of the International Council of Scientific Unions (COSPAR) to provide the scientific community throughout the world with a means of exploiting the capabilities made available by the new space techniques and to stimulate the participation of scientists in that field.

In addition to the unions and COSPAR, there are four committees with space research activities or that use observations from satellites: the Scientific Committee on Antarctic Research (SCAR), the Scientific Committee on Problems of the Environment (SCOPE), the Scientific Committee on Oceanic Research (SCOR), and the Scientific Committee on Solar-Terrestrial Physics (SCOSTEP). SCOPE is primarily concerned with the use of space techniques for monitoring and surveying natural resources. It has also carried out some studies on the possibility of monitoring environmental parameters from space platforms. The Committee on Science and Technology in Developing Countries (COSTED) was created in 1966 to provide assistance to developing countries. The Inter-Union Commissions on Frequency Allocations for Radio Astronomy and Space Science (IUCAF) and on Radio Meteorology (IUCRM) are active in encouraging studies using a variety of space techniques.

INTERNATIONAL ASTRONOMICAL UNION

IAU was founded in 1919 to associate astronomers all over the world in order to develop astronomy through international cooperation and promoting its study in all the areas involved. A number of those areas had previously been the responsibility of various international groups, such as the Union of Solar Studies, the International Latitude Service, the International Time Association, and others.

The activity of the union is reflected in the structure of the forty commissions formed by the General Assembly in order to pursue the scientific objectives of the union. Their activities include the study of special branches of astronomy, the encouragement of collective investigation and the discussion of issues relating to international agreements and standardization. The commissions enjoy a large degree of autonomy under the direction of commission presidents and vice-presidents, assisted by organizing committees.

The commissions of IAU are the following: Euphemerids; Documentation and Astronomical Data; Astronomical Telegrams; Celestial Mechanics; Positional Astronomy; Astronomical Instruments; Solar Activity;

Radiation and Structure of the Solar Atmosphere; Atomic and Molecular Data; Physical Study of Comets; Minor Planets and Meteorites; Physical Study of Planets and Satellites; Rotation of the Earth; Position and Motions of Minor Planets, Comets, and Stars; Comets and Satellites; Light of the Night Sky; Meteors and Interplanetary Dust; Photographic Astrometry; Stellar Photometry and Polarimetry; Double and Multiple Stars; Variable Stars; Galaxies; Stellar Spectra; Stellar Radial Velocities; Time, Structure, and Dynamics of the Galactic System; Interstellar Matter; Stellar Constitution; Theory of Stellar Atmospheres; Star Cluster Associations; Exchange of Astronomers; Radio Astronomy; History of Astronomy; Close Binary Stars; Astronomy from Space; Stellar Classifications; Teaching of Astronomy; Cosmology; High Energy Astrophysics; Interplanetary Plasma and the Heliosphere; Protection of Existing and Potential Observatory Sites; Search for Extraterrestrial Life; and Working Group on Planetary System Nomenclature.

INTERNATIONAL UNION OF GEODESY AND GEOPHYSICS

IUGG was formed in 1919 to promote the study of problems relating to the shape and physics of the Earth. It has seven international associations, five of which have specific interests in space science:

- International Association of Geodesy (IAG)
- International Association of Geomagnetism and Aeronomy (IAGA)
- International Association of Hydrological Sciences (IAHS)
- International Association of Meteorology and Atmospheric Physics (IAMAP)
- International Association of Physical Sciences of the Oceans (IASPO)

The activities of the union and of the above associations in the space field include the holding of symposia, the issuance of publications, the maintenance of committees or commissions to deal with specific topics, the adoption of resolutions and recommendations, and the participation in the planning of the major research programs of ICSU.

INTERNATIONAL UNION OF RADIO SCIENCE

URSI was established as a union in 1919 and was one of the founding members of the International Research Council (now ICSU). The member committees of URSI, of which there are thirty-eight, are formed under the auspices of the academies of science or the corresponding organizations in their respective territories. The union has the following nine commissions: Electromagnetic Meteorology, Fields and Waves, Signals and Systems, Electronic and Optical Devices and Applications, Electromagnetic Noise and Interference, Wave Propagation and Remote Sensing, Ionospheric Radio and Propagation, Waves in Plasmas, and Radio Astronomy.

SCIENTIFIC COMMITTEE ON ANTARCTIC RESEARCH

SCAR was set up in 1958 by ICSU and is in charge of furthering the coordination of scientific activity in the Antarctic. In fostering programs of circumpolar scope and significance in all appropriate scientific disciplines, SCAR works closely through ICSU bodies and in the field of space research and maintains liaison with COSPAR. Membership of SCAR is comprised of interested international bodies and nations actively engaged in research in the Antarctic.

Of interest to SCAR are ground-based observations in Antarctica that are related to space research. Among the areas involved are upper-atmosphere physics, geomagnetism, meteorology, geodesy and cartography, and glaciology. Studies related to space research are included in the program of each of these disciplines, with the major interest lying in upper-atmosphere physics and meteorology. The activities in each of the above disciplines are coordinated by permanent working groups. The Upper Atmosphere Working Group, for example, is concerned with research covering the ionosphere, cosmic rays, the aurora, etc. The techniques employed include the use of visual observations, all-sky cameras, photometers, ionosondes, and occasional rocket soundings. Use is also made of data from geodetic satellites, recorded at some Antarctic stations. Most ships operating in Antarctic waters use satellite navigation systems, and the pictures of the distribution of ice and cloud cover obtained from meteorological satellites aids route selection for ships and aircraft.

SCIENTIFIC COMMITTEE ON OCEANIC RESEARCH

SCOR, created by ICSU in 1957, has a Working Group on Remote Measurement of the Oceans from Satellites. The committee studies the possibility of using information from some of the satellites in experiments such as the Typhoon Operational Experiment and the Ocean Color Imager.

SCIENTIFIC COMMITTEE ON SOLAR-TERRESTRIAL PHYSICS

SCOSTEP was created in 1978 by ICSU for the purpose of promoting, planning, organizing, and coordinating interdisciplinary programs in solar-terrestrial physics. The following steering committees of SCOSTEP are responsible for the development and oversight of organized interdisciplinary programs in their respective fields of expertise:

- Middle Atmosphere Program (MAP);
- Monitoring the Sun-Earth Environment (MONSEE);
- Solar Maximum Analysis (SMA); and
- Solar-Terrestrial Physics-Meteorology.

INTER-UNION COMMISSION ON FREQUENCY ALLOCATIONS FOR RADIO ASTRONOMY AND SPACE SCIENCE

In 1960, the commission was formed to secure protection from interference for a number of channels of radio frequencies that are required for radio astronomy and space science research. It comprises representatives of URSI, IAU, and COSPAR and meets periodically. The commission discusses the technical merits of radio requirements and submits proposals to ITU with a view to securing an adequate allocation of frequency channels suitably distributed throughout the spectrum.

The space research requirements are for frequencies suitable for transmission from a satellite to the Earth in order to communicate the results obtained with appropriate measuring equipment carried in the satellite. Protection from interference is also required for the frequencies used to determine accurately the continuously changing position of the satellite in its travel through space. For radio astronomy, a series of frequencies is required at approximately harmonic intervals. The need for highly accurate allocation of frequencies arises from the fact that the experimental techniques used today in both radio astronomy and space research are extremely sensitive to radio interference.

INTER-UNION COMMISSION ON RADIO METEOROLOGY

IUGG and URSI set up the commission in 1959 to study those aspects of meteorology that affect the propagation of electromagnetic waves in the Earth and planetary atmospheres and the application of electromagnetic techniques to meteorology.

FEDERATION OF ASTRONOMICAL AND GEOPHYSICAL SERVICES

The federation, established by ICSU in 1956, consists of nine services. Each service acts as an international center for the collection and preliminary processing, on a long-term basis, of many kinds of geophysical and astronomical data. Each service works under the scientific direction of a directing board, appointed by one or more of the cooperating unions: IAU, IUGG, and URSI. The directing boards determine the type of data to be collected and the format of publication to be used.

The processing in a central location of the data received from observatories in many countries ensures a high degree of homogeneity in the published data. Uninterrupted series of homogeneous data extending over long periods of time are also required for certain types of scientific research. The services help to maintain the desired continuity.

GLOBAL ATMOSPHERE RESEARCH PROGRAM

The first GARP global experiment, known as Global Weather Experiment (GWE), took place from December 1, 1978, to November 30, 1979. Observations were made by using five geostationary satellites, two polar-orbiting satellite systems, traditional ground-based observing systems, and several new observing platforms on aircraft, balloons, ships, and drifting buoys. The experiment has led to new methods of data assimilation and analysis in operational weather forecasting. These advances, along with increased computer power, have brought substantial improvements in the range and accuracy of weather forecasts.

WORLD CLIMATE RESEARCH PROGRAM

The basic goals of WCRP can be divided into three specific objectives of climate research, each of which necessitates extended observations using space platforms. They are the following:

- To establish the physical basis for the prediction of weather anomalies on time scales of one to two months. This effort requires observing the initial values of the ocean surface temperature and sea ice fields.

- To predict the variations of the global climate over periods of up to several years.
- To characterize climate variations over periods of several decades and assess the potential response of climate to other natural or manmade influences such as pollution.

PANEL OF WORLD DATA CENTERS

World data centers collect data for the following disciplines: glaciology, meteorology, oceanography, rockets and satellites, solar-terrestrial physics disciplines, solid-Earth geophysics disciplines, and marine geology and geophysics. Each WDC is responsible for: a) collecting a complete set of data in the field for which it is responsible; b) safekeeping of the data; c) copying and reproduction of data; c) supplying copies to other WDCs; and d) preparation of catalogues of all data in its charge. Operating expenses for WDCs are met by the sponsoring national institution in each host country and by charges to users.

COMMITTEE ON SPACE RESEARCH OF THE INTERNATIONAL COUNCIL OF SCIENTIFIC UNIONS (COSPAR)

COSPAR was established by ICSU in 1958 to continue the cooperative programs of satellite and rocket research undertaken during IGY (1957–1958). It is an interdisciplinary scientific committee concerned with scientific research. Its objective is to promote the progress of all kinds of scientific research in which space vehicles, rockets, and balloons are used. The goals of the organization are to be achieved through the development of space research programs by the international community of scientists working through ICSU and adhering national scientific institutions and international scientific unions.

The activities of COSPAR in regard to scientific programs have a consultative and coordinating character and are based on existing national programs and joint international projects. COSPAR also provides a forum for the presentation of the most significant scientific studies in space research. Regular sessions of COSPAR Interdisciplinary Scientific Commissions (ISCs) allow scientists from all over the world to exchange results and help define the state of knowledge in specific areas of research. COSPAR is also requested by other international bodies to conduct certain studies on defined subjects or to contribute to the information exchange process. Other activities include organizing, in collaboration with other competent international bodies, specialized symposia and workshops.

In 1982 the COSPAR Panel on Space Research in Developing Countries was reorganized. In addition to organizing symposia and workshops, COSPAR financially supports the participation of many scientists from developing nations. The panel has taken a number of initiatives directed at identifying and setting up a few programs to promote space research in developing countries.

Twelve of the international scientific unions federated in ICSU are members of COSPAR. Representatives of those unions, together with seven elected members, form the COSPAR Executive Council, which is responsible for the definition of the scientific policy of the committee. Several unions are also represented on COSPAR interdisciplinary scientific commissions, ensuring in this way close interactions in areas of mutual interest.

COSPAR maintains close contacts with a number of other ICSU bodies, such as SCOSTEP, IUCAF, SCOPE, SCOR, and International Ursigram and World Days Service. There is a continuing exchange of information between COSPAR, IAF, and IAA. COSPAR is also in close collaboration with WMO through the joint organization of a number of scientific symposia. Through its membership in IUCAF, COSPAR maintains contacts with ITU. The European Space Agency continues to maintain close links with COSPAR, taking an active part in the meetings and deliberations of the interdisciplinary scientific commissions. COSPAR provides expert technical advice to the United Nations and has observer status with the Committee on the Peaceful Uses of Outer Space. It furnishes the United Nations with annual reports on progress in space research and conducts, on request, studies on specific topics.

INTERNATIONAL ASTRONAUTICAL FEDERATION

The main activity of IAF and its associated bodies, the International Academy of Astronautics (IAA) and the International Institute of Space Law (IISL),[112] is to organize congresses and scientific meetings, undertake studies on specific topics related to astronautics, and publish the results of those activities. IAF consists of societies and institutions in different countries. It encourages participation of national scientists and organizations of individuals from countries where no astronautical societies exist.

The annual congresses of IAF deal with certain aspects of research and engineering. Several symposia organized by IAA and a colloquium organized by IISL are usually held within the framework of the congress. The activities of IAF have grown with the evolution of astronautics itself and its committees have been enlarged and modified accordingly. All meetings of IAF and its associated bodies are open to participants from all nations.

INTERNATIONAL SPACE UNIVERSITY ORGANIZATION

ISU is a nonprofit, nongovernmental international institution that offers graduate programs in space-related education. The first educational institution of its kind, ISU was founded in 1987 to provide graduate students and young professionals with summer session programs embracing a broad range of study in a multidisciplinary approach to space education. ISU is pursuing the goal of establishing a permanent campus system comprising a central campus and a network of affiliate campuses in existing centers worldwide. ISU has been designed to become a leading-edge educational program, providing the finest facilities and resources available for outer space studies. In 1991, ISU had 137 students from twenty-seven nations and more than 140 faculty and visiting lecturers from fourteen countries.[113]

Chapter Five

The World of Satellites

The space age may be said to have begun with the orbiting of Sputnik 1 by the USSR in October 1957. The launch of Sputnik 1 took the world by surprise, especially because it was the Soviet Union and not the United States that had taken this first, glamorous step into space. The United States reacted by establishing a number of committees to deal with aeronautics development. The U.S. Army was given permission to orbit an Earth satellite and new life was injected into the Navy's faltering Vanguard program, begun in 1955. By January 1958, a small Explorer 1 was sent into orbit by the Army. The National Aeronautics and Space Administration was also established. Many hundreds of satellites have since been sent into space. The former USSR, Britain, France, and Canada have developed satellites for a number of purposes. The former USSR has tended to group most of its unmanned satellite launches under the Cosmos program. Britain has concentrated on the Ariel series of ionospheric research satellites, while the Canadians have cooperated on the International Satellite for Ionospheric Studies project by developing the Alouette satellites for measuring electron-density distribution and variation in the ionosphere, and cosmic variation flux. Mainland China, Germany, Italy, Japan, Australia, and India have launched satellites with their own or another country's rockets.[114]

Satellites can be of various types according to the function they are supposed to serve. Earth observation is one of the main uses of satellites today. Viewing the Earth from space emphasizes, perhaps more than any other perspective, the global nature of our environment and its sensitivity to change from both natural and manmade sources. Earth observation, or remote sensing, has already contributed substantially to improved use of the environment.

Communications are by far the most important of satellites applications. Stationed over the Equator, geostationary spacecraft orbit the Earth at the same speed and in the same direction as the Earth itself rotates on its axis. They can therefore act as permanent links between different parts of the Earth. Communications satellites have special characteristics that distinguish them from other transmission media such as coaxial cables, optical fiber, and radio links. When communicating between fixed points, they make it possible to connect points located across considerable distances. Also, the fact that they allow both multiple access—from the ground to the satellite—at the transmitting end and multiple destinations—from the satellite to the ground—at the receiving end, makes the switching of these links simple. Satellites lend themselves well to handling mobile-serving communications, as with ships at sea. Satellites are an ideal vehicle for distributing and disseminating information. The potential of satellites for direct broadcasting is great and vast improvements can be expected over the coming years in the areas of high image definition, large-screen projection, electronic printing of newspapers, and the distribution of data among home computers.

National security interests around the world are increasingly dependent on satellites. Satellites for remote sensing allow effective and simultaneous monitoring of large areas of territory. Communications satellites assist in the coordination of air, sea, and ground forces through reliable links between those forces and central commands. For those reasons, a large part of the investment to develop satellite technology comes and will continue to come from the military services of wealthy nations.

SATELLITE ORGANIZATIONS

International Telecommunications Satellite Organization. INTELSAT is a nonprofit cooperative of 120 countries[115] that owns and operates the global communications satellite system—a system used by more than 180 countries, territories, and dependencies for international communications and by twenty-seven countries for domestic communications. Two-thirds of the world's international telephone service and virtually all international television broadcasting are carried via INTELSAT satellites.[116]

The organization has a four-tier structure that consists of the following elements:

1. The Assembly of Parties is composed of representatives of the governments of the member countries of INTELSAT and is the principal organ. It meets every other year to consider recommendations presented to the Meeting of Signatories and the Board of Governors concerning implementation of general policies and long-term objectives of the organization. Each party, or country, has one vote at the meeting;

2. The Meeting of Signatories, composed of either the member governments themselves or their designated telecommunications entities, meets annually to consider issues related to the financial, technical, and operational aspects of the system;

3. The Board of Governors, which is the executive arm of INTELSAT, is composed of representatives of the signatories whose investment share meets or exceeds the minimum share for membership on the board as determined annually by the Meeting of Signatories. The minimum is calculated so that there are between twenty and twenty-two members of the board, exclusive of members representing groups from the five regions defined by the ITU. The board meets four times each year and decisions are usually reached by consensus;

4. The Executive Organ, consisting of about 630 people from some sixty countries, runs INTELSAT on a day-to-day basis. The INTELSAT staff includes engineers, accountants, and individuals with expertise in the fields of procurement, public and external relations, law, and training.

INTELSAT operates under two interrelated international agreements: the INTELSAT Agreement, concluded among governments, and the Operating Agreement, concluded among governments or their designated telecommunications entities. Membership is open to any state that is a member of ITU.

Since INTELSAT began providing service in 1965, the amount of full-time telephone traffic carried on the INTELSAT system has increased 800-fold, while the charges for these services have decreased dramatically. Virtually every country in the world uses the INTELSAT system for international public telephone service. Multinational corporations utilize the system for a variety of business communications, both internal and external. Intracorporate business satellite networks transmit management, marketing, and training information, introduce new products, and facilitate long-distance operation. Large banking and investment companies utilize the networks for electronic funds transfers. Millions of dollars, marks, and yen are sent in seconds electronically from one continent to another. Travelers rely on flight and reservation information provided through networks utilizing the INTELSAT system to transmit technical, commercial, and administrative information essential to airline operations around the world. Overseas purchases and hotel payments are verified and authorized through points-of-sale credit transaction networks.[117]

Before 1965, live transoceanic television broadcasting was impossible. After INTEISAT launched its first satellite, Early Bird, live news and special event programs became realities. In 1969 it was possible for the world to watch the most exciting achievement of the twentieth century: mankind's first steps on the Moon. INTELSAT also made the 1988 Summer Olympics in Seoul and the 1990 World Soccer Cup in Italy the most widely viewed events in history. Global demand for all kinds of broadcasting continues to grow unabated—international, regional, and domestic.

The earth stations accessing the INTELSAT system are the essential links for global connectivity and global service. These earth stations are owned and operated by telecommunications organizations around the world. INTELSAT establishes the technical and operational requirements that these earth stations must meet to access the cooperative system. In turn, each INTELSAT user country is responsible for compliance with these requirements. An earth station antenna can be as high as a ten-story building or as small as a telephone booth. The INTELSAT Operations Center is the hub of system operations and the focus for all ground network activities. It manages and monitors access by all earth stations to assist earth-station operators in meeting their service needs.[118]

The INTELSAT system is the most extensive and reliable communications network in the world with more than 2,200 earth station links. Fifteen satellites in geostationary orbit provide continuous communications coverage over virtually the entire globe. Each generation of spacecraft has applied advanced technology and introduced better ways of providing service. Over the past twenty-seven years, INTELSAT has developed seven different satellite series. Service is currently provided by a combination of INTELSAT V/V-A and INTELSAT VI satellites. The newest generation of satellites, INTELSAT VII, is under construction and will introduce additional flexibility into spacecraft operations. The INTELSAT Satellite Control Center (SCC) is responsible for management and maintenance of the satellite fleet. Through a network of tracking, telemetry, command, and monitoring earth stations located strategically around the world, the SCC remains in constant contact which each satellite to ensure that it is functioning properly. The SCC also plays a vital role in the launch of INTELSAT satellites, overseeing and commanding their deployment to geostationary orbit.[119]

International Organization of Space Communications. INTER-SPUTNIK was established to meet the demand of various countries for telephone and telegraph communications, exchange of radio and television programs as well as transmission of other kinds of information via satellite, in order to promote political, scientific, economic, and cultural cooperation. The INTERSPUTNIK Foundation Agreement was signed in November 1971 and came into force in July 1972.[120]

Each nation member of INTERSPUTNIK has the right to explore and use outer space on an equitable basis. Cooperation is to be based on the principles of mutual respect, sovereignty, independence, equality, and noninterference in the internal affairs of other states. INTERSPUTNIK is an open international intergovernmental organization. Its supreme governing body is the board, consisting of representatives of the member states. Sessions of the board are held at least once a year. The permanent executive and administrative body of INTERSPUTNIK is the directorate headed by the director-general. Financial activities of the organization are supervised by the auditing committee.

Since January 1983 INTERSPUTNIK has been operating on a commercial basis. While the organization is still in existence at this time, given the political changes in the member countries in the last two years, its future is uncertain.

International Maritime Satellite Organization. INMARSAT was established to meet the needs of international shipping for reliable communications. On the initiative of IMO, an International Conference on the Establishment of an International Maritime Satellite System was convened in 1975–1976. Two independent international instruments, the Convention on INMARSAT and the Operating Agreement, were adopted by the conference in September 1976, and entered into force in July 1979.

The purpose of INMARSAT is to make provision for the space segment necessary for improving maritime communications, thereby assisting in improving communications for distress and safety of life at sea, efficiency and management of ships, maritime public correspondence services, and radiodetermination capabilities. The organization either owns or leases the space segment and seeks to serve all geographical areas where there is a need for maritime communications. Its space segment is open for use by ships of all nations.

INMARSAT, headquartered in London and accorded the legal capacities of a corporate body, has a legal personality and is responsible for its own obligations. It is afforded limited protection for its global services from competitive regional or national systems. The organization possesses distinctive characteristics as an intergovernmental organization. It is managed by both private and public entities, and it has an obligation to provide a public telecommunications system while also operating as an economically viable organization. Its structure represents a permanent working relationship on the international level between governments and commercial entities.

The essential components of the INMARSAT system, which permits telephone, telex, facsimile, and data communications between ship and shore and ship to ship via satellite, are the following:

- The INMARSAT space segment, which consists of the satellites and support facilities leased or purchased by INMARSAT. The space segment includes operational and spare satellites in geostationary orbit over each of the three main ocean regions;
- The Coast Earth Stations (CESs), which provide the connection among the space segment and the national and international fixed telecommunications networks and are owned and operated by individual signatories:
- The Network Coordination Stations (NCSs), which are leased by INMARSAT in each ocean region and which assign space segment capacity to SESs and CESs as required;
- The Ship Earth Stations (SESs), satellite communication terminals that are purchased or leased by the users of the system;
- The Operation Control Center (OCC) at INMARSAT headquarters, which monitors and coordinates all operational activities in the INMARSAT network.[121]

European Telecommunications Satellite Organization. The basic function of EUTELSAT is the design, development, construction, operation, and maintenance of the space segment of the European telecommunications satellite systems. The organization's prime objective is the provision of the space segment required for international public telecommunications services in Europe.

EUTELSAT was created in May 1977 by seventeen European telecommunications administrations or recognized private operating agencies of the European Conference of Postal and Telecommunications Administrations (CEPT). The organization had provisional status in 1977 and attained its definitive form on September 1, 1985, upon the entry into force of an Intergovernmental Convention and an Operating Agreement, signed by twenty-six European states. The organization is headquartered in Paris.[122]

European Organization for the Exploitation of Meteorological Satellites. EUMETSAT is an intergovernmental organization of sixteen European states. Its primary objective is to establish, maintain, and exploit European systems of operational meteorological satellites. The legal basis for the organization is the Convention, an agreement among the sixteen member states that gives EUMETSAT legal personality. The organs of EUMETSAT are the Council of the member states and the director who oversees a Secretariat. The organization is funded by contributions from member states.

The council, the supreme body of EUMETSAT, comprises delegates from all sixteen member states and meets about three times per year. Each member state has one vote. Major decisions have to be taken unanimously or with a two-thirds majority also representing two-thirds of the financial contributions. The council guides the general policy of EUMETSAT and its financial commitments. The director is responsible for the implementation of the decisions of the council and is the legal representative of EUMETSAT. The director heads a small secretariat located at headquarters in Darmstadt, Germany.

Among the functions of EUMETSAT are the following:

- Imaging the Earth in three spectral bands from Meteosat;
- Disseminating digital imagery to Primary Data User Stations;
- Disseminating analogue imagery and other data to Secondary Data User Stations;
- Relaying of images from the USA GOES geostationary satellite;
- Deriving and distributing meteorological products from the Meteosat image data;
- Collecting and distributing observational data from remote sites, through the Meteosat Data Collection System;
- Operating the Data Relay System for rapid distribution of data;
- Operating the new Meteorological Data Distribution Mission;
- Monitoring the development, by ESA and industry, of the new satellites of the Meteosat Operational Program;
- Preparing for new programs in line with the EUMETSAT Long-Term Plan;
- Overall responsibility for support of USA polar-orbiting satellites through equipment installed in Lannion, France, and operated by the Météorologie Nationale.[123]

Arab Satellite Communication Organization. ARABSAT was formed in April 1976 by the members of the Arab League to serve the interests served by the national post and telecommunications administrations that coordinate their efforts in the Arab Telecommunication Union (ATU).

The main purpose of ARABSAT is to establish and maintain a regional telecommunications system for the Arab region. The system is intended to fulfill the aspirations of the Arabs in establishing their own regional satellite system as a means for socioeconomic development of the region and for paving the way for technology transfer. ARABSAT serves as a complement to the terrestrial network for routing regional public telecommunications traffic among main international switching centers and provides new possibilities for television program exchange among Arab countries.

The main organs of ARABSAT are the following:

1. The General Assembly, which is composed of all ARABSAT Ministers of Post, Telephone, Telegraph, and Telecommunications and meets once a year. Its functions include the review of ARABSAT activities and general policy and to make recommendations to the board of directors;

2. The Board of Directors, composed of representatives of nine member states. Of these, the five that hold the most shares are permanent, while four are elected by the General Assembly every two years;

3. The Executive Organ, headed by the director-general, who is the chief executive and legal representative of the organization and is responsible to the board. The Executive Organ, composed of a number of administrative units, carries out the day-to-day activities of the organization.

The ARABSAT space segment is composed of two satellites located on the geostationary orbit and a third that serves as spare. Those satellites are designed to be launched either on the European Ariane or the U.S. space shuttle. Ground facilities, including earth stations are set up to be compatible with the ARABSAT space segment. A control network consists of a primary control station located in Dirab near Riyadh and a secondary station situated near Tunis.[124]

Communication Satellite Corporation. COMSAT is a partly private, partly government-owned corporation established by the U.S. Congress in the Communications Satellite Act of 1962 as the agency to spearhead the opening of the international satellite communications era. COMSAT later became a leading member of INTELSAT.

Tongasat. Tongasat is a company based on Tonga, a small island-state in the South Pacific. It is run by an entrepreneur on behalf of the kingdom of Tonga. Tongasat has been allocated six orbital slots that cover a broad swath of Asia, ranging from India to the west coast of the United States, but does not currently own or operate any satellites. Tongasat is negotiating to gain access to one of Russia's orbiting Gorizont satellites, which have six C-band transponders and one Ku-band transponder. Tongasat has allegedly agreed to allow another company to use two of its six orbital slots.[125] While Tongasat is a small entity and its deals are limited in scope, the case is interesting because it is an example of dealings in orbital slots, which is illegal in the United States but not regulated elsewhere.

MILITARY SATELLITES

As noted above, national security concerns around the world are increasingly dependent on the use of satellites. Operational U.S. military communications satellites began with the launch of Tacsat in 1969 by the Department of Defense to provide service to both ships and airplanes. Fleet Satellite Communications (FLTSATCOM) satellites are the spaceborne portion of a worldwide U.S. Navy, Air Force, and Department of Defense communications system linking naval aircraft, ships, submarines, ground stations, the Strategic Air Command, and the Presidential Command Network. Four spacecraft form the constellation required for continuous global coverage. [126] Leasat, a series of four geosynchronous satellites for relay, serving U.S. Navy ships, is leased by the Department of Defense and is also used by the U.S. Army, Marine Corps, and Air Force. Leasat can be placed in orbit only by the U.S. space shuttle. At least until the next decade, the constellation of communications satellites used by the Department of Defense should remain largely unchanged. However, satellites are scheduled to be fine tuned by adding refinements such as additional capabilities useful to tactical military commanders. The Defense Department has recently been examining the schedule for the so-called Defense Satellite Communications System Replenishment. Like the current spacecraft, the replenishment satellites would provide jam-resistant communications. The goal is to have extremely high frequency communications because those are the most difficult for an enemy to jam or intercept.[127]

The Milstar system, formally known as the Military Strategic and Tactical Relay System, is built by Lockheed Missiles and Space of Sunnyvale, California. It is to include as many as 4,000 ground terminals and is intended to provide the military with a jam-resistant encoded communication system that would function even during a nuclear conflict. The Milstar system, satellites to be orbited by the mid-1990's, will provide both extremely high frequency and UHF communications. The NATO III network, operated by the NATO Integrated Communication System (NICS), began in 1970 to provide voice, telegraph, and data services to eligible military and civilian authorities of NATO.

The Soviet Union has launched since 1970 several hundred clusters of eight military communications satellites into near-circular random orbits. The low orbit allows use of small low-power ground terminals, and interception of signals is difficult for other nations.

Chapter Six

Societies, Foundations, and Institutes

The *American Institute of Aeronautics and Astronautics* (AIAA) is the world's largest professional society devoted to the progress of engineering and science in aviation and space. For over sixty years, the institute has been the principal voice and information resource for aerospace engineers, scientists, managers, policy makers, students, and educators. Since 1963, most American achievements in flight have been made by AIAA members. The institute has 40,000 members. One of the main functions of AIAA is to meet the information needs of its members. It is one of the world's most complete and up-to-date information resources. AIAA publishes periodicals, six journals, technical papers, and books. It has an online database and bibliographic services.

The *National Space Society* is an educational, nonprofit membership organization promoting space exploration, development, research, and human habitation. NSS has more than 22,000 members and 120 chapters situated throughout the United States and in more than forty other nations. Those chapters sponsor regional meetings, educational symposia, and the annual International Space Development Conference. They serve as local organizers for space education and political activism, and frequently provide speakers for schools, civic organizations, and other forums on the merits of space science, exploration, and education. One of the major goals of NSS is to raise public support for space. Leaders and members of the society are frequently cited in newspaper articles and editorials and often appear on radio and television news to raise the attentiveness of the space-interested public, in the space-related activities of government, industry and academia.[128]

The *Space Frontier Society of New York* is a prospace advocacy group in the New York City area. It is one of the most active chapters of the National Space Society. The SFS is also closely associated with the *Space Studies Institute*, a private nonprofit research group in Princeton, NJ, working to open the resources of space for human benefit. SSI is developing and demonstrating the tools and techniques needed to build large, useful structures in space, using materials already outside of the Earth's gravity well such as those available from the Moon. The Space Frontier Society is also associated with the *Space Frontier Foundation*, a New York space-advocacy organization.

Spacecause was formed in 1987 to provide grass-roots political support for the civilian space program. Since then, it has promoted the expansion of the human species into space. As the prospace watchdog on Capitol Hill, Spacecause monitors and analyzes all legislation for its space impact. Among its activities, Spacecause has fought to prevent the cancellation by Congress of the space station program, lobbied Congress to protect the integrity of NASA's budget, defended the budgets of agencies that support space commercialization in the departments of Transportation and Commerce, and played a role in the drafting and passage of the Space Settlement Act.

The *American Space Council* (ASC) is an educational membership organization with the express purpose of "creating a spacefaring civilization with communities beyond the Earth in our lifetime." More specifically, ASC promotes the LUNA 2010 initiative: 100 people living on the Moon by the year 2010.

The *British Interplanetary Society* was formed in 1933 as a wholly independent and self-governing learned society for promoting the study and development of astronautics. The society is a registered charity. It was incorporated as a company limited by guarantee and in 1945 became the national society of the United Kingdom for astronautics. It was a founding member of the International Astronautical Federation (IAF). Membership is open to those interested in astronautics and the society's work without regard to technical or other qualifications. From the 1950s to the present, total membership has been in the range of 3,000 to 4,000 with two-thirds residing in the United Kingdom.

Other organizations of the type of those described above are: the *Planetary Society*, the *United States Space Foundation*, the *American Astronautical Society*, the *National Space Club*, the *Space Generation Foundation*, and the *Washington Space Club*.

Among the institutions that deal with space law there are the following:

International Institute of Space Law. Located in Paris, the institute was founded by the International Astronautical Federation in 1960. The IISL replaced the Permanent Committee on Space Law, which the IAF had created in 1958. The current president is a member of the International Court of Justice. Since 1958 the IISL has held over thirty annual colloquia on space law in many nations. It currently has 400 members who are distinguished for their contributions to space law development. While the IISL is a component of the International Astronautical Federation, it functions autonomously in accordance with its charter.

The purposes and objectives of the institute include the cooperation with appropriate international organizations and national institutions in the field of space law, the carrying out of tasks for fostering the social science aspects of astronautics, space travel and exploration, the organization of meetings and colloquia on juridical aspects of space sciences, and the publication of proceedings, reports and other releases.

The governing body of the institute is the board of directors, which consists of the president, the presidents emeriti, two vice-presidents, the secretary, the treasurer and eleven other IISL members elected as directors. The General Meeting of Members convenes once a year during the Colloquium.

The income of the institute consists of contributions from individual members, organizations, and the sale of the institute's annual "Proceedings of the Colloquium on the Law of Outer Space."[129]

International Institute of Air and Space Law. The institute, headquartered at Leiden University in the Netherlands, was officially established by the Minister of Transport and Public Works of the Netherlands on March 17, 1986.

The purposes and objectives of the institute are to:

- conduct and promote research in the field of air and space law;
- issue publications on air and space law;
- create a center of up-to-date information of developments in air and space law;
- to teach air and space law to all interested parties;
- to contribute to the safe and economic operation of international air transport services and to carry out space activities.

Among the functions of the institute are those of collecting and studying literature on air and space topics; organizing courses, seminars, symposia, and conferences; maintaining contacts with persons and institutions committed to the objectives of the institute; and realizing projects related to air and space law on a national or international scale.[130]

The European Centre for Space Law. The center was established on May 12, 1989, at the European Space Agency headquarters in Paris. The goals of ECSL are to:

- promote the knowledge of the law relating to space activities;
- encourage interdisciplinary exchanges between lawyers, engineers, economists, and scientists;
- encourage university research in certain topics related to space law;
- provide for exchange of information and ideas through the organization of colloquia and by the dissemination of information.

Under the charter of ECSL, membership is open, without charge, to Europeans. The European Space Agency, which is also a member, provides an annual bursary for young lawyers involved in space law research.

The center is not a new institute or research establishment attached to a localized body. It is not a library, gives no classes, and awards no degrees. It has no legal personality. ECSL is an informal structure drawing together all those wishing to take part in examining and proposing principles for European Space Law. The Charter of the Center is itself a loose, informal document designed to suit the needs of a forum rather than an organization proper.

The ordinary administration of the center is the task of the ECSL's Paris office in the main office building of the European Space Agency. This office is made up of the ECSL chairman, the deputy chairman, and the secretariat. The chairman oversees the development of ECSL activities and maintains a close liaison with board members regarding future projects. The deputy chairman acts as coordinator for the content of ECSL NEWS which is edited and published by the ESA publications division. The secretariat has one permanent member of staff, the ECSL secretary, who is a lawyer and information systems expert. The secretary is responsible for the day-to-day administration and the preparation of ECSL activities, including workshops and board and general meetings of the center. The board members are in charge of: compiling laws and regulations; university relations; colloquia and workshops; ECSL publications; external publications affairs; and finance. As the nations of Europe draw closer together, the center can be an important tool for the coordination of national laws regulating aerospace activities.[131]

Notes

1. *Encyclopedia Americana*, 1988 Edit., vol. 25, p. 357.
2. *Ibid.*, p. 358.
3. *Encyclopedia Americana*, supra, vol. 1, pp. 226–228.
4. See *United States Government Manual*, Office of the Federal Reporter/National Archives and Records Administration, Washington, DC., 1991/92 Edit., p. 635 et seq.
5. See *NASA Spinoff*, 1991, p. 8.
6. *Ibid.*, p. 12.
7. *Ibid.*, pp. 16–17.
8. *Ibid.*, p. 18.
9. *Ibid.*, p. 22 et seq.
10. *Ibid.*, p. 28 et seq.
11. *Ibid.*, p. 30 et seq.
12. *Ibid.*, p. 36.
13. *Ibid.*, p. 56.
14. By reorganization plan No. 4 of 1970 (5 U.S.C. app.). Its principal functions are authorized by title 15, chapter 9, United States Code (National Weather Service); title 33, chapter 17, U.S.C. (National Ocean Survey); and title 16, chapter 9 U.S.C. (National Marine Fisheries Service).
15. See *United States Government Manual*, supra, p. 161.
16. *Ibid.*, p. 452.
17. *Ibid.*, p. 431.
18. *Ibid.*, p. 565 et seq.
19. U.S.C. 15; 21; 47; 35; 151.
20. 47 U.S.C. 701–744.
21. See National Space Council, 1990 *Report to the President*, p. 8.
22. See *United States Government Manual*, supra, p. 237.

23. *Ibid.*, p. 241.

24. *Ibid.*, pp. 249–250.

25. *Ibid.*, pp. 251–252.

26. *Ibid.*, p. 253.

27. A more detailed list of NASA responsibilities is contained in Executive Order 12333 of December 4, 1981.

28. See *Defense News*, April 13, 1992, p. 24.

29. James Bamford, *The Puzzle Palace*, New York: Penguin Books, 1984, p. 249.

30. *Space News*, April 4, 1992, p. 18; *Defense News*, April 14, 1992, p. 24.

31. *Ibid.*, June 11, 1992.

32. See *United States Government Manual*, supra, p. 256.

33. See article by James Hacket, *The Washington Times*, April 21, 1992, p. 3.

34. See article by George Melloan, *The Wall Street Journal*, February 10, 1992, p. A17.

35. 42 U.S.C. 1861–1875.

36. See *Guide to Programs*, Fiscal Year 1992, National Space Foundation, p. 30 et seq.

37. The following is a summary of information contained, among other sources, in ESA publication f-05 of March 1989, and the 1990 Annual Report of ESA.

38. For more information see the *Report on Activities* 1989/90 of the Austrian Space Agency.

39. The following chapter is a summary of the May 1989 publication of the Science Policy Office and issues 1 through 10 of Space Connection, an information service of the Ministry for Scientific Policy, as well as other Belgian government publications.

40. See *Qualité Espace*, international issue, March 1992, Nos. 18 and 19, p. 9 et seq.

41. *Space News*, April 13, p. 4.

42. *Ibid.*, July 7, 1992, p. 1.

43. See publication PR 2/290 A: DLR 2./2 of the German Aerospace Research Establishment.

44. See publication of DARA GmbH, Konigswinterer Strasse, W-5300 Bonn 3.

45. *Ibid.*

46. *Ibid.*

47. See publication VO-PR 2/91 C:DLR 2./1 of the German Aerospace Research Establishment.

48. See *Space News*, April 6, 1992, p. 30.

49. *Ibid.*, March 16, 1992, p. 6.

50. For details on the structure of the Italian Space Agency and related organs, see Law 186 of May 30, 1988.

51. See *Space News*, March 16, 1992, p. 9.

52. For more information, see *Ruimtevaart*, June 1990, published by The Netherlands Space Society.

53. Information obtained from the Ministry of Public Works and Transports, General Directorate for Telecommunications, General Subdivision of Networks and Telecommunications Systems.

54. For further information, see *Switzerland in Space*, report by the Federal Space Affairs Advisory Commission, April 1986; and *Europe in Space . . . what about Switzerland?*, a publication of the Directorate for International Organizations, Federal Office for Education and Science.

55. See *Britain in Space*, a publication of the British National Space Centre, March 1991.

56. See official publication of the Natural Environment Research Council on Remote Sensing Applications Development Unit.

57. See *Space Research at Rutherford Appleton Laboratory*, published by the Science and Engineering Research Council.

58. See *BNSC Space News*, Summer 1991, p. 10.

59. Information provided by the Ministry of Education and Research, Department of Research.

60. For more information, see the *Annual Report* of the Norwegian Space Center, 1991, and *Norway Exports '88, Space Technology and Services*, published by the Export Council of Norway in Cooperation with the Norwegian Space Center.

61. The section on Sweden is a summary from the *Sweden in Space* publication of the Swedish National Space Board of 1990.

62. The following is a summary of an article by V. Kopal in *ECSL News*, the *Bulletin of the European Center for Space Law*, published under the auspices of the European Space Agency.

63. See article by Plaviciosu in *ECSL News* supra.

64. See *Bulletin of the European Centre for Space Law*, published under the auspices of the European Space Agency.

65. See "Salute to Salyut" in *LIFTOFF*, vol. 1, Spring 1992, pp. 17–23.

66. See *Space News*, September 14, p. 1.

67. *Ibid.*, April 6, 1992, pp. 1 and 28.

68. *Ibid.*, August 24, 1992, p. 3.

69. *Ibid.*, February 10, 1992.

70. *Ibid.*

71. *Ibid.*, August 17, 1992, p. 11.

72. *Ibid.*

73. *Ibid.*, August 10, 1992, pp. 4 and 21.

74. *Ibid.*

75. See *Space in China, Launch Services & Space Technology*, a publication of China Great Wall Industry Corporation, p. 2 et seq.

76. See *Remote Sensing in China*, a publication of the National Remote Sensing Center, State Science Technology Commission of China, printed for distribution at the World Space Congress, August 28–September 5, 1992.

77. See the official publication of NASDA (National Space Development Agency of Japan), 1991.

78. For more information, see *Space in Japan*, 1991–92, prepared by the Research and Development Bureau, Science and Technology Agency.

79. See *Canada in Space: 25 years and counting*, a publication of the National Research Council of Canada, 1987.

80. See the *Annual Report of the Canadian Space Agency*, 1990–91, III.

81. *Ibid.*, p. 1 et seq.

82. *Ibid.*, p. 3.

83. *Ibid.*, p. 5.

84. This chapter is a summary of the *Australian Space Report to Cospar for 1990–1992*, by the Australian National Committee for Solar Terrestrial and Space Physics of the Australian Academy of Science, July 1992.

85. See *Space News*, May 11, 1992, p. 18.

86. *Ibid.*, p. 14.

87. *Ibid.*, p. 11.

88. See *Report of the Committee on the Peaceful Uses of Outer Space* to the General Assembly, official records for the forty-sixth session, supplement No. 20(A/46/20).

89. U.N. doc. A/AC.105/514, April 20, 1992.

90. See *Space Activities of the United Nations and International Organizations*, United Nations publication A/AC.105/358, January 1986, p. 9 et seq.

91. U.N. doc. A/AC.105/244.

92. *Ibid.*

93. See *Report of the Scientific and Technical Subcommittee on the Work of its Twenty-Ninth Session*, U.N. doc. A/AC.105/513, March 10, 1992.

94. See *Space Activities of the United Nations and International Organizations*, supra, pp. 21 et seq.

95. *Ibid.*, p. 29 et seq.

96. *Ibid.*, pp. 31–32.

97. See *United Nations Handbook*, published in 1990 by the Ministry of External Relations and Trade of New Zealand.

98. *Space Activities of the United Nations*, supra, p. 46 et seq.

99. *Ibid.*, p. 44.

100. *Ibid.*, p. 44.

101. *Ibid.*, pp. 39–42.

102. See *Space Activities of the United Nations*, supra, p. 50 et seq.

103. *Ibid.*, p. 63 et seq.

104. *Ibid.*, pp. 68–69.

105. The organization formally came into existence on April 7, 1948.

106. See *Space Activities of the United Nations*, supra, pp. 70–71.

107. *Ibid.*, p. 73.

108. *Ibid.*, p. 77 et seq.

109. *Ibid.*, p. 95 et seq.

110. For more information on INMARSAT, see chapter 5.

111. See *Space Activities of the United Nations*, supra, pp. 164–198.

112. For more information on IISL, see chapter 6.

113. See *Annual Report* of the International Space University, pp. 1–6.

114. See *Encyclopedia Americana*, supra, vol. 24, pp. 286–287.

115. See *INTELSAT Report* 1990–1991, p. 37.

116. *Space Activities of the United Nations*, supra.

117. See INTELSAT publication 1/04/6336E of 1991.

118. *Ibid.*

119. *Ibid.*

120. *Space Activities of the United Nations*, supra, p. 148.

121. *Ibid.*, p. 154.

122. *Ibid.*, p. 160.

123. See EUMETSAT Annual Report, 1990.

124. *Space Activities of the United Nations*, supra, p. 160.

125. See *Space News*, March 30, 1992.

126. The description of military satellites is, in part, a summary from "Communication Satellite" in *Encyclopedia Americana*, supra, vol. 7, p. 433.

127. See *Space News*, September 14, 1992, p. 8.

128. See Fact Sheet of the National Space Society.

129. See publication of the International Institute of Space Law of the International Astronautical Federation, August 1992.

130. See descriptive pamphlet published by the International Institute of Air and Space Law, Leiden University, The Netherlands.

131. See the *European Centre for Space Law Biennial Report 1989–91*, ESA BR-77, pp. 3–4.

Index

About the Author

GEORGE V. D'ANGELO is an attorney in private practice. For several years he worked for the Office of Legal Affairs of the United Nations where he was Assistant Secretary to the Legal Subcommittee of the Committee on the Peaceful Uses of Outer Space. He specializes in international law, high technology, and aerospace, with particular regard to financing, procurement, joint ventures, and acquisitions.